ASEAN–CHINA COOPERATION FOR ENVIRONMENTAL PROTECTION AND SUSTAINABLE ENERGY DEVELOPMENT

Series on Asian Regional Cooperation Studies

Print ISSN: 2717-5456
Online ISSN: 2717-5464

Track II Diplomacy usually refers to an unofficial process with a government background. It plays an important role in promoting regional cooperation in Asia. The main tasks of Track II Diplomacy are to analyze problems, make policy recommendations, and provide intellectual support for official cooperation. Participants are mainly experts and scholars engaged in policy research as well as the government officials participating in their private capacities. The Institute of Asian Studies (IAS) at China Foreign Affairs University is China's focal point for three most influential Track II mechanisms of this region, namely the Network of East Asian Think-tanks (NEAT), the Network of ASEAN-China Think-tanks (NACT) and the Network of Trilateral Cooperation Think-tanks (NTCT). IAS is proud to launch Series on Asian Regional Cooperation Studies jointly with the World Scientific Publishing, the most reputable English academic publisher in Asia. The purpose of this series is not only to motivate more scholars to get involved in Track II Diplomacy of Asia, but also to increase the recognition of the three networks by reaching out to a wide audience. Based on the platforms of NEAT, NACT and NTCT, this series will invite outstanding scholars to conduct in-depth research on significant and challenging issues in Asian regional cooperation, through conference proceedings, scholarly monographs, textbooks and translations with high academic standards and strong policy relevance.

Published

Vol. 3: *ASEAN–China Cooperation for Environmental Protection and Sustainable Energy Development*
edited by YANG Yue and LI Fujian

Vol. 2: *Case Studies on Preventive Diplomacy in the Asia-Pacific*
edited by GUO Yanjun and WU Lin

Vol. 1: *Preventive Diplomacy in the Asia-Pacific*
edited by GUO Yanjun and LI Fujian

Series on Asian Regional Cooperation Studies—Vol. 3

ASEAN–CHINA COOPERATION FOR ENVIRONMENTAL PROTECTION AND SUSTAINABLE ENERGY DEVELOPMENT

Edited by

YANG Yue

LI Fujian

China Foreign Affairs University, China

World Scientific

NEW JERSEY • LONDON • SINGAPORE • BEIJING • SHANGHAI • HONG KONG • TAIPEI • CHENNAI • TOKYO

Published by

World Scientific Publishing Co. Pte. Ltd.
5 Toh Tuck Link, Singapore 596224
USA office: 27 Warren Street, Suite 401-402, Hackensack, NJ 07601
UK office: 57 Shelton Street, Covent Garden, London WC2H 9HE

Library of Congress Cataloging-in-Publication Data
Names: Yang, Yue, 1976– editor. | Li, Fujian, 1986– editor.
Title: ASEAN-China Cooperation for Environmental Protection and Sustainable
Energy Development / edited by Yue Yang, Fujian Li, China Foreign Affairs University, China.
Description: New Jersey : World Scientific, [2021] | Series: Series on Asian regional cooperation studies, 2717-5456 ; Vol. 3 | Includes bibliographical references.
Identifiers: LCCN 2020040369 | ISBN 9789811221798 (hardcover) |
ISBN 9789811225222 (ebook) | ISBN 9789811225239 (ebook other)
Subjects: LCSH: Energy policy--Environmental aspects--Southeast Asia. | Energy policy--Environmental aspects--China. | Energy development--Environmental aspects--Southeast Asia. | Energy development--Environmental aspects--China. | Environmental protection--Southeast Asia. | Environmental protection--China. | Southeast Asia--Foreign economic relations--China. | China--Foreign economic relations--Southeast Asia.
Classification: LCC HD9502.A7852 A84 2021 | DDC 333.720959--dc23
LC record available at https://lccn.loc.gov/2020040369

British Library Cataloguing-in-Publication Data
A catalogue record for this book is available from the British Library.

For any available supplementary material, please visit
https://www.worldscientific.com/worldscibooks/10.1142/11866#t=suppl

Desk Editors: George Vasu/Lixi Dong

Typeset by Stallion Press
Email: enquiries@stallionpress.com

https://doi.org/10.1142/9789811225222_fmatter

Foreword

The Network of ASEAN–China Think-tanks (NACT) was proposed in 2013, and officially launched in 2014. NACT is the only Track II mechanism focusing on promoting ASEAN–China relations recognized and supported by the governments of ASEAN members and China. Five years have passed since its establishment. With unswerving support and substantial contribution from ASEAN NACT members, remarkable progress has been made within just five years. NACT has built a solid three-level working mechanism including Country Coordinators' Meeting (CCM), Working Group Meeting, and Annual Conference. On 3 July 2014, the first NACT CCM was held in Beijing, which adopted NACT Concept Paper, and established the principles, purposes, and operation mechanism of NACT. On 4 July, the Seminar on Building a China–ASEAN Community of Common Destiny and Launching Ceremony of Network of ASEAN–China Think Tanks was held by China Foreign Affairs University in Beijing. Within the NACT framework, a network of "NACT China" research bases has taken shape, and their research work has started. In November 2014, Premier Li Keqiang made it clear in East Asian leaders' meetings that NACT should give a full play of their positive roles and pool wisdom for Asian cooperation.

By the end of 2019, NACT successfully convened eight working group meetings, six country coordinators meetings, and six annual conferences on a wide range of issues of common concern. The outcomes of joint researches and meetings have been submitted to both the respective governments of ASEAN countries and China through each member's own channel, which makes important intellectual contributions and supports building a much closer ASEAN–China relation. Also, by the end of 2019, about 100 policy recommendations proposed by both ASEAN and China scholars have been submitted to official levels of both sides for consideration. NACT's work has been highly recognized by the governments, businesses and academia in the region. Vice foreign minister of the host country and other senior officials attended and addressed the NACT Annual Conference of each year. In 2018 and 2019, NACT outcomes have been successfully submitted to the 21st and 22nd ASEAN–China Summit and noted in both Third Progress Report on the Implementation of the 2016–2020 Plan of Action to Implement the Joint Declaration on the ASEAN–China Strategic Partnership for Peace and Prosperity and Chairman's statement of the 21st and 22nd ASEAN–China Summit.

In order for NACT joint research to reach out to a much wider audience, it was approved by all NACT Country Coordinators in the fifth NACT Country Coordinators Meeting co-hosted by NACT Singapore and NACT China on 20 December 2018 that NACT should start to publish joint researches of all Working Groups from 2019. This book is a collection of research papers contributed by ASEAN and China scholars who attended NACT Working Group Meeting on Regional Cooperation for Sustainable Energy Development co-hosted by NACT Vietnam and NACT China on 16 April 2019 and NACT Working Group Meeting on Environmental Protection in ASEAN and China on 17 May 2019.

ASEAN–China energy cooperation has a solid and broad basis because of the comparative economic advantage between them. The energy trade between ASEAN countries and China can be dated from 1978 when the Philippines and China signed a long-term crude oil trading agreement. After the end of the Cold War, especially from the beginning of the 21st century, both sides strengthened their energy cooperation continuously and achieved fruitful results with the rapid development of the ASEAN–China Free Trade Area. Today, the Belt and Road Initiative covers all ASEAN countries geographically and also involves many energy cooperation sectors. Considering the geographical proximity of the ASEAN countries, the Chinese government is paying more attention to the energy cooperation with ASEAN countries. China's new round of open-door policies, with particular focus on its relations with ASEAN countries, provides energy cooperation with governmental support. Against such a backdrop, expanding bilateral energy cooperation especially cooperation for sustainable energy development requires wisdom from policymakers, academicians and practitioners.

Cooperation on environmental protection is also an important and integral part of the regional efforts for sustainable development. Both ASEAN and China have strong political will to promote environmental protection cooperation. However, given the development gap, countries at different development levels place environmental issue differently on the policy agenda. In this sense, we are still facing some common challenges, such as environment and development concerns and institutional mechanisms for cooperation and so on and so forth.

On both vital and relevant aforementioned topics, the contributing scholars give their ingenious and insightful thoughts from either national or regional perspective. Two NACT Working Group Reports are also incorporated in the appendices of this book including innovative and practical policy recommendations on strengthening ASEAN–China sustainable energy and environmental protection cooperation in existing priority areas and identifying new priority areas. If readers use it to debate the relevant issues of our day, this book will have made its mark. With unswerving support from all NACT members who are highly devoted to healthy and sustainable ASEAN–China relations, NACT will continuously endeavor to organize working group studies and produce high quality research outcomes and forward-looking and feasible policy recommendations so as to better serve ASEAN and China governments and peoples as well.

To make this book possible, deep thanks first go to all the contributing authors for their precious time and great efforts. During the long journey to publication, we could not have wished for better and more supportive editors than World Scientific and we have been fortunate to work with them. This book is a product of NACT. It is fitting to dedicate this book to all NACT members. They are in alphabetical order: NACT Brunei (Brunei Darussalam Institute of Policy and Strategic Studies), NACT Cambodia (Cambodian Institute for Cooperation and Peace), NACT Indonesia (Universitas Gadjah Mada of Indonesia), NACT Laos (Institute of Foreign Affairs of the Lao PDR), NACT Malaysia (Institute of Strategic and International studies of Malaysia), NACT Myanmar (Myanmar Institute for Strategic and International Studies), NACT Philippines (Foreign Service Institute of the Philippines), NACT Singapore (East Asian Institute at National University of Singapore), NACT Thailand (Thai Ministry of Higher Education, Science, Research and Innovation), NACT Vietnam (Diplomatic Academy of Vietnam), and NACT China (China Foreign Affairs University).

Yang Yue and Li Fujian
April 2020

https://doi.org/10.1142/9789811225222_fmatter

About the Editors

Yang Yue is an Associate Professor and the Deputy Director of the Institute of Asian Studies at the China Foreign Affairs University. She received her PhD in International Relations from the Chinese Academy of Social Sciences. She has been a Fulbright Scholar at Georgetown University from 2006 to 2008. She studies American politics and foreign policy. She has published books and a series of papers on the political process of American social movements, American electoral politics and the US foreign policy toward the Asia-Pacific region. She is currently conducting research on the US Asia-Pacific policy and cultural diplomacy. She also leads courses in "Contemporary American Government and Policy" and "Approaches and Topics in American Politics." As a member of the Network of ASEAN–China Think-tanks (NACT China), she has also been actively engaging in Track II diplomacies.

Li Fujian is a Research Fellow at the Institute of Asian Studies, China Foreign Affairs University. Fujian obtained his first degree in Business Administration from Shandong University (China) as well as an MSc in International Business from the University of Birmingham (UK), and a PhD in Political Science and International Relations from the University of Western Australia. Fujian has been an Adjunct Research Fellow with the Center for Oceanian Studies at Sun Yat-sen University since 2013. Fujian's research interests are centered on China's regional relations and Sino-Australian relations.

https://doi.org/10.1142/9789811225222_fmatter

Contents

https://doi.org/10.1142/9789811225222_0001

Chapter 1

Cambodian Strategy for the Development of Energy: Current Progress and Future Prospect

Panharith Long

Cambodian Institute for Cooperation and Peace, Cambodia

Introduction

Over the last two decades, Cambodia's economy has grown profoundly with the streak of 7% of GDP growth annually and this has made it a new lower middle-income country in 2015.[1] In the near future, Cambodia is anticipated to change its status from a lower middle-income country to an upper-middle income country by 2030

[1] Sodeth Ly, "Cambodia is Now a Lower-middle Income Economy: What Does This Mean? East Asia & Pacific on the Rise," August 11, 2016, accessed March 15, 2019. http://blogs.worldbank.org/eastasiapacific/cambodia-is-now-a-lower-middle-income-economy-what-does-this-mean.

and to become a high-income country by 2050.[2] By far, it is undeniable that the energy sector is one among many other main sectors that has played an enormous role in elevating the living standard of the Cambodians as it is one of the main sources of production line.

At present, only around 69% of the population has access to electricity, which implies that about 5 million Cambodians still have no access to grid electricity and are dependent on car batteries, wood, and other traditional fuels for energy.[3] Furthermore, merely 62% of households use firewood, 5% use charcoal, 31% use liquefied petroleum gas, and 2% use electricity for cooking.[4] Yet, to a further extent, the high cost of electricity in the country causes the access to be unaffordable to the poor while constraining the comparative advantage or economic competitiveness and discouraging investment.

With the understanding that the energy services are essential to economic activity, social development and quality of the population's lives, the Royal Government of Cambodia has outlined its key priorities which include the increase of energy access, reduction of the cost of energy and increasing the energy reliability and security for the country.[5] Alongside, the government also takes into account considerably the side effects that could be caused by the energy development to the environment and society as the country is also a party to the Paris Agreement, negotiated at the 2015 United Nations Climate Change Conference.[6]

---

[2] "Cambodia Aims to Become 'Developed Country' by 2050: PM," *Xinhua*, March 15, 2018, accessed April 14, 2019. http://www.xinhuanet.com/english/2018-03/15/c_137041624.htm.

[3] In 2017, 69% of the households had access to grid-connected electricity. See Electricity Authority of Cambodia, *Salient Features of Power Development in Kingdom of Cambodia*. Phnom Penh: EAC, 2018.

[4] World Bank, *Cambodia — Beyond Connections: Energy Access Diagnostic Report Based on the Multi-Tier Framework (English)*. Washington, D.C.: World Bank Group. https://openknowledge.worldbank.org/handle/10986/29512.

[5] H. Pheakdey, *Toward a Low Carbon Energy Transition in Cambodia*. Phnom Penh: Enrich Institute, 2018.

[6] Phal Niseiy Sao, "Cambodia's Path to Fulfill the Paris Climate Agreement," *Mekong Eye*, July 17, 2017, accessed March 15, 2019. https://www.mekongeye.com/2017/07/15/cambodias-path-to-fulfill-the-paris-climate-agreement/.

Current Progress

The Cambodian energy sector has experienced a huge transformation with an astronomical progress in the past decades. Back in 2007, Cambodia consumed about 1.5 GWh and approximately 85% of the energy consumption was powered entirely by diesel and heavy fuel oil (HFO) in isolated mini-grids.[7] A decade later, in 2017, the energy consumption has undergone a fivefold increase, which was about 8.2 GWh, and more importantly the source of generation has shifted from oil and HFO to coal and hydroelectricity, predominantly.[8] The tremendous increase in the energy consumption has occurred as the government has engineered and built the gridline of transmission and distribution that is accessible to the public. More so, the government has also improved the capacity of the domestic generation with the electrification program both to urban and rural areas, at the end of 2017; 81% of all villages and about 68.5% of all households were connected to the powerline or the national grid.[9] The National Grid is the main distribution channel of electricity within the country, receiving electricity from local and foreign power plants. To date, the national grid distributes to 30 substations covering areas of 19 provinces and cities. By 2020, the National Grid Master Plan commits the government to extending coverage to all 25 provinces and cities of Cambodia.

Electricity generation in Cambodia is divided into two main sources: domestic and imported. And back then, the rising energy demand in Cambodia was firstly fulfilled by the imported electricity from its neighboring countries, namely, Vietnam, Thailand and Laos. The import was at its peak between 2010 and 2012 when it shared more than 60% of the total consumption. Nevertheless, the amount of electricity import started to drop when Cambodia put the

---

[7] 3i Cambodia, "Cambodian Energy Sector: Overview of Potential Electricity Sector Opportunities," 2018.

[8] *Ibid.*

[9] Cheng Sokhorng, "Kingdom More Energy Independent, Business, Phnom Penh Post," Kingdom More Energy Independent, Business, *Phnom Penh Post*, January 05, 2018, accessed March 15, 2019. https://www.phnompenhpost.com/business/kingdom-more-energy-independent.

hydropower dam and the coal-fired power plant in place and eventually the amount of import has dropped to 16.67%, which was 442 MW of 2650 MW at the end of 2018.[10]

By 2016, with the combination of hydropower (930 MW, 55%), coal (429 MW, 26%), diesel/HFO (305 MW, 18%), and biomass (18 MW, 1%), Cambodia had a total generation capacity of 1.68 GW.[11] Furthermore, in 2017, another 135 MW of coal capacity and a 10 MW solar farm also became operational; in addition to that, the Lower Sesan II Dam was also inaugurated with full capacity of 400 MW in 2018.[12] The contribution of electricity generation from hydropower and coal are currently at the same level, 46.8% and 43.7%, respectively. However, even though the capacity of the generation from the dam doubles that from coal, the production from hydro dams is sufficient only in the rainy season; meanwhile, during the dry season the production falls significantly because there is less water available in reservoirs.

With the production of hydropower growing, Cambodia, in 2017, was able to meet fully the energy demand by its own generation during the rainy season. However, during the dry season it still relies on import, mainly from Vietnam, to cover the deficit and also to secure the daytime demand and for grid stabilization. Phnom Penh, the capital, and its surrounding areas accounted for about 70% of the overall demand of the national energy consumption, with this approximately a total of 200 MW of peaking power plants which are fueled by diesel and HFO located in the city.[13]

---

[10] Vannak Chea, "Cambodia Has Wind Energy Potential — Study," *Khmer Times*, March 12, 2019, accessed March 20, 2019. https://www.khmertimeskh.com/50585976/cambodia-has-wind-energy-potential-study/.

[11] Electricity Authority of Cambodia, *Report on Power Sector of the Kingdom of Cambodia 2017 Edition*. Phnom Penh: EAC, 2017.

[12] Koemsoeun Soth, "Lower Sesan II Dam Opens, National, Phnom Penh Post: Lower Sesan II Dam Opens, National," *Phnom Penh Post*, December 18, 2018, accessed March 20, 2019. https://www.phnompenhpost.com/national/lower-sesan-ii-dam-opens.

[13] 3i Cambodia, "Cambodian Energy Sector: Overview of Potential Electricity Sector Opportunities," 2018.

Sector strategy

The government's national strategy for growth is set out in the Rectangular Strategy Phase IV, 2018–2023, which applies to the sixth term of the National Assembly, 2018–2023.[14] Improving the energy sector is an objective of the Rectangular Strategy Phase II — economic diversification. The Rectangular Strategy Phase IV will realize through the National Strategy Development Plan (NSDP) 2019–2023, which is still on draft. Moreover, specifically, for the energy sector, according to Cambodia's National Energy Sector Development Policy, the government has its main goal to strive for an adequate, affordable, and sustainable energy supply in support of economic development.

As the NSDP 2019–2023 is still on draft, the NSDP 2014–2018 is the main instrument that could demonstrate the government's energy development strategy. The National Strategic Development Plan 2014–2018 stressed that despite the progress in expanding electricity, price cuts and institution strengthening, the further development of the energy sector is crucial for increasing competitiveness and sustainable economic growth.[15] The Government's eight main energy policy objectives in the National Strategic Development Plan are as follows:

(1) Further expand the low cost and high energy generation capacity, especially from renewable energy sources, along with the development of all levels of transmission lines to strengthen energy security and ensure high-efficiency electricity supply and distribution. Quality is reliable and affordable to meet the development needs.
(2) Encourage the private sector to invest in electricity generation and transmission and distribution infrastructure, focusing on technical and economic efficiency and mitigating environmental and social impacts.

---

[14] International Relations Institute of Cambodia, Rectangular Strategy Phase IV. http://iric.gov.kh/rectangular-strategy-phase-iv-in-khmer/.
[15] Cambodia National Strategic Development Plan, 2014–2018. http://www.cdc-crdb.gov.kh/cdc/documents/NSDP_2014-2018.pdf.

(3) Accelerate the implementation of rural and urban electrification strategy (par. 81–90) in order to achieve the goal that all villages in Cambodia will acquire electricity from national grid or other sources by 2020.
(4) Further support the Rural Electrification Fund to assist the acquisition of electricity for the population through Electricité du Cambodge (EDC) funds and other government budget allocation as well as financial support from development partners.
(5) Pursue rationalization measures for electricity consumption by reducing power tariffs during off-peak hours to serve production and irrigation systems aimed at improving agricultural productivity and accelerating the development of the industry and handicraft sectors.
(6) Enhance the exploration and commercialization of the oil and gas sector, which is the resource for Cambodia's economic development in the long term and also shares a tremendous potential for energy security.
(7) Strengthen the institutional capacity, human resources, planning and management of the energy sector.
(8) Continue to actively participate in energy cooperation under the Greater Mekong Subregion Framework.[16]

Furthermore, in line with the Industrial Development Policy (IDP) 2015–2025, the government has cut down the electricity costs for a specific industrial zone and has expanded transmission networks to increase supply reliability.[17] The government has indicated challenges of industrial growth in the IDP, including that the high cost of electricity and shortages of supply make the domestic and foreign investors reluctant to invest in Cambodia. By far, IDP also calls for a review of the forecasts on the long term of energy demand and supply in order to achieve the economic and industrial development goals.

---

[16] *Ibid*.
[17] Cambodia Development Policy 2015–2015. http://www.mih.gov.kh/File/UploadedFiles/12_9_2016_4_29_43.pdf.

Key institutions and sector investment opportunities

EDC is a state-owned electricity supplier under the Ministry of Mines and Energy and Ministry of Economy and Finance. The agency manages the purchase, transmission, and distribution of electricity through the country. In fact, EDC is the only institution that has power over Cambodia's full power supply. Besides, three government agencies including Ministry of Mines and Energy, Electricity Authority of Cambodia (EAC), and EDC have worked together to reduce the cost of electricity through the 2015–2020 electricity price priority plan. The electricity price is $0.18 per kilowatt-hour for residential users and $0.16 per kilowatt-hour for major industrial users. By 2017, the government provided $51 million in loans nationwide to reduce electricity costs for low-income households.[18]

Furthermore, electricity in Cambodia is run by two types of licensees: (i) independent power producers (IPPs) and (ii) consolidated licensees.[19] On the one hand, the IPPs hold the license to generate electricity and sell it to the supplier, for instance, EDC, or industries via the Purchasing Power Agreement. On the other hand, the consolidated licensees which are EDC and other Rural Electricity Enterprises (REEs) generate electricity to the consumers that are connected to their distribution line. In addition, there are two types of licensees that can transmit electricity: (i) the national transmission licensee, EDC, which has the right to supply the distribution network across the country; and (ii) the special purpose licensees, which have the right to own, operate, and manage the identified transmission facilities for delivering and selling electricity in bulk.

As of 2016, 90.9% of power generation capacity (producing 97.5% of total energy) in Cambodia was owned by IPPs, with a further 2.35% of generation capacity being owned by private companies operating isolated generation and distribution systems. Most IPPs are either fully owned by international investors and developers or set up as JV companies between local companies and international

[18] Netherlands worldwide (2018). Energy in Cambodia.

[19] ADB, *Cambodia: Energy Sector Assessment, Strategy, and Road Map*, 2018.

investors/developers. The majority of investment to date has come from China with other investments from Japan, Malaysia, and Vietnam.

Apart from the above, regarding the investment prospect, there are a number of investment opportunities in the energy sector in Cambodia. Besides this, for instance, as part of rural electrification fund, hydropower plants and solar power systems are entitled to receive subsidies of up to 25% of the total investment cost.

Moreover, especially for solar energy, Cambodia has some of the best solar-energy resources in the region due to high radioactivity. Based on the finding, the Kingdom has an area of around 134,500 square kilometers, which has the potential for solar power development by photovoltaic (PV).[20] Regarding wind power, the geography of Cambodia makes it possible to install wind turbines in the southern part of Tonle Sap, a mountainous region in the southwest and coastal areas such as Preah Sihanouk, Kampot, Kep, and Koh Kong, with annual average wind speed of 5 meters per second or higher. The total land area is about 5%.[21] For hydropower (GC), the country's geographical conditions provide a favorable environment for such construction, especially on the country's southwestern plateau.[22]

Moreover, as a predominantly agricultural nation, there is in Cambodia a ready availability of agricultural by-products such as rice husks and maize residue. Biomass generated from by-products can be an accessible source of energy as the inputs are readily available. Besides this, biogas generated from animal waste also plays an important role as a source of energy.

Constraints and challenges

Nevertheless, Cambodia is also facing several constraints and challenges hindering its energy development, which include (i) Fragmented Power Grid and Electricity Supply; (ii) Heavy Reliance on Hydropower

[20] Victor Jona, *Scaling Solar in Cambodia*. 2018.

[21] Pheakdey Heng, *Toward a Low Carbon Energy Transition in Cambodia*. Phnom Penh: Enrich Institute, 2018.

[22] Victor Jona, *Scaling Solar in Cambodia*. 2018.

and Coal; (iii) Lack of Financial Resources for Grid Development; (iv) Limited Access and Slow Connection Process to a Reliable Electricity Supply; (v) Limited Institutional and Human Resource Capacity for Power Sector Development.[23]

Currently, the electricity grid in Cambodia is still unintegrated. Yet, a fully integrated nationwide network would allow EDC to provide power from one area to another and manage its spare capacity as a reserve to optimize the network performance. Besides, there is a disparity in electricity price between the areas that receive energy from the grid line and those areas that are not connected and thus the price there is more. As of 2017, aside from EDC, there were about 366 REEs licensed by the EAC to distribute electricity to its connecting network.[24] Anyhow, though the government could oversee the process of licensing of electricity distribution from the EAC and has the objective to cover 100% of villages by 2020, up until now there is no least cost electrification plan that determines the mix of grid extension and off-grid.[25]

Moreover, in accordance with the 2015 Power Development Plan, it has called for more large hydropower and coal-fired power plants adding to the generation through 2030.[26] The plan is aimed to shift the diesel and oil-fired generation and to rely less on import. However, the coal- (GC) fired power plant and the large hydropower dam bring along a myriad of impacts including environmental, social, and operational problems. For instance, the coal plant has emitted a number of gases such as carbon dioxide and other harmful substances including nitrogen oxide and sulfur oxide into the atmosphere.

Besides that, economically, as Cambodia is not a producer, it has relied fully on the import of the product, which leaves it vulnerable to price fluctuation and supply constraints. Similarly, regarding

---

[23] ADB, *Cambodia: Energy Sector Assessment, Strategy, and Road Map*, 2018.

[24] Electricity Authority of Cambodia, *Report on Power Sector of the Kingdom of Cambodia 2018 Edition*. Phnom Penh: EAC, 2018.

[25] ADB, *Cambodia: Energy Sector Assessment, Strategy, and Road Map*, 2018.

[26] Power Development Plan. http://open_jicareport.jica.go.jp/pdf/11675097_03.pdf.

hydropower, the construction and the structure itself could cause severe detrimental impacts to the fisheries and agricultural land, and also force the locals to relocate. Further, the reservoir of the dam also causes another environmental issue which is the source of the emission of methane gas into the atmosphere, to some extent, contributing to the greenhouse gases that effect climate change.[27]

Furthermore there are several issues that have been caused by the operation of hydropower and coal-fired plants which more specifically are related to the supply and demand of energy. The production capacity of hydropower varies conforming to the season. During the rainy season, as there is sufficient water flow, the dam could provide excess generation. However, during the dry season, as there is a shortage of water, the dam also generates less electricity, which causes a supply shortage. Besides, as Cambodia has a decline of demand during nighttime, there is also excess generation caused by the inflexible coal power plant as it can only reduce output by shutting down.

Additionally, as EDC is primarily responsible for the expansion of the medium transmission line, in recent years, it has installed the high and low- (GC) voltage lines with the support from development partners. More so, EDC is also easing to enhance public and private partnerships in renewable energy projects. However, based on the estimation of the Asian Development Bank, EDC is facing about $600 million of financial gap between 2016 and 2021.[28] EDC could only fill this gap with its financial resources, financing from development partners, motivating private investment, and seeking further annual budget support from the National Budget. The financial constraint for grid development also affects REEs because many enterprises cannot afford to expand the low-voltage gird yet and need subsidies to support the connection to rural areas.

Furthermore, according to the 2018 report of the World Bank's Doing Business, it has showed that the process of accessing electricity

---

[27] Bobby Magill, "Hydropower May Be Huge Source of Methane Emissions," *Climate Central*, October 29, 2014, accessed March 19, 2019. https://www.climatecentral.org/news/hydropower-as-major-methane-emitter-18246.

[28] ADB, *Cambodia: Energy Sector Assessment, Strategy, and Road Map*, 2018.

is also slow.[29] For the newly constructed building or factory, in order to obtain electricity supply, it would take around 79 days. To fully elaborate, EDC requires 75 days to issue a clearance for a new connection and 63 days to complete the external connection work, including electricity meter installation. This long process, plus the high cost of an electricity connection, contributes to lower electrification rates than in neighboring countries.

Additionally, EDC's ability to increase clean energy production through the private sector, public and private partnerships is still limited. EDC needs further experience to enhance competitive bidding in a structured approach that requires standard tender documents, power purchasing agreement samples, and developed procedures for reviewing investment proposals.

Ways Forward

The energy development in Cambodia is headed in the right direction. Nevertheless, in order to achieve its target, Cambodia has to improve its strategy by developing further physical infrastructure.

- Reducing costly electricity imports has helped reduce the cost of supply. Besides, Cambodia has to continue to expand its electricity grid and complete electricity agendas to bring modern energy services to the whole population and further lower electricity prices on par with its neighbors.
- In addition, emphasis on industry-wide energy conservation — including the use of electricity and fuel for transport and cooking — is essential to prevent rising demand, reducing reliance on coal and other fossil fuels. This approach could set Cambodia on the path of low carbon development.
- Further, Cambodia should continue to accelerate the shift from overreliance on hydropower and coal to other affordable renewable energy sources such as solar plants and wind energy. Renewable energy sources, such as solar energy, can complement hydropower

[29] World Bank, Doing Business 2018: Reforming to Create Jobs, 2018.

by meeting the daily requirements and covering the lack during the dry season when the reservoir has limited supply.

- In addition, there is a possibility to develop floating solar energy panels on current hydropower reservoirs, which could reduce large-scale use of land, transmission lines and terminals or substations for solar farms. By diversifying electricity supplies with basic renewable resources, Cambodia energy security would be secured.
- Besides, subsidies are also required to help poor households pay for the grid connection costs. Through grants to the rural electrification fund, EDC and development partners are providing subsidies to rural households and electricity licensees for increased electrification.
- More so, to reach its 2030 goals, the intense participation from both government and private sector is needed, for the development of institutional capacity, human resources, and also the planning and management of the energy sector.

https://doi.org/10.1142/9789811225222_0002

Chapter

2

The Current State and the Prospects of Waste Management in Cambodia

Panharith Long

Cambodian Institute for Cooperation and Peace, Cambodia

Introduction

Rapid economic and population growth in Cambodia is leading to heavy environmental pollution. As the urban expansion is not well planned, the infrastructure is substandard and inadequate to absorb the waste generated from the rapidly expanding households, industries, and commercial activities. The wastes are poorly managed due to underfinanced and unreliable collection services that are resulted from insufficient and poorly maintained equipment, unsanitary and indiscriminate disposal, the burning of wastes by residents who are reluctant to pay the collection fee and the lack of awareness about proper waste disposal. The rising waste production and improper treatments have led to severe impacts on the environment; in consequence, how to properly collect and manage waste is an issue that needs to be addressed. This chapter, based on the secondary data analysis, examines the current state of waste management in Cambodia, striving for solutions, recommendations, and possible investment opportunities.

Current State of Waste Management in Cambodia

Cambodia produces approximately 10,000 tons of waste, including municipal solid waste, industrial, medical, and constructional wastes every day with only about 20% being recycled. Phnom Penh, the capital city, generates the most wastes with a number ranging from 2,000 to 3,000 tons per day with 600 tons of plastic.[1] However, the information on waste management for the country as a whole is limited since most of the studies are only targeted at Phnom Penh.

Municipal solid waste management

Municipal solid waste or urban solid waste, in accordance with the Sub-Decree on Urban Solid Waste Management, refers to the wastes that are generated from the residents, services, or commercial activities, which do not contain toxic or hazardous substances. The provincial or municipal authorities are responsible to carry out the municipal solid waste management within their own areas.[2] Most of the provincial authorities are partaking in contracts with a private company to collect the municipal waste. For Phnom Penh, the municipality has reached an exclusive agreement with CINTRI with the term of

[1] Van Vichar, "Cambodia Produces 10,000 Tons of Waste Every Day: Summit," *VOD*, September 20, 2019, accessed October 1, 2019. https://vodenglish.news/cambodia-produces-10000-tons-of-waste-every-day-summit/; See also UNDP Cambodia, "*Our Plastic Problem is Out of Control. Here's How We Can Fight It,*" June 7, 2018, accessed 29 November, 2018. http://www.kh.undp.org/content/cambodia/en/home/presscenter/articles/2018/our-plastic-problem-is-out-of-control–here-s-how-we-can-fight-i.html. According to the ACRA Foundation, around 10 million plastic bags are used in Phnom Penh every day. Urban Cambodians use more than 2,000 plastic bags every year.

[2] Royal Government of Cambodia. Sub-Decree on Garbage and Urban Solid Waste Management, Pub. L. No. 113 (2015).

49 years since 2002.[3] CINTRI sustains its cost of operation by collecting service fees through electricity bills.[4]

Under the estimation, Phnom Penh generates about 4 million tons of municipal solid waste per year, with an average generation from a household of 0.73 kg per day.[5] The municipal solid waste of Phnom Penh is from households (55.3%), hotels/guesthouses (16.7%), restaurants (13.8%), markets (7.5%), shops (5.4%), and offices (1.4%).[6] In addition, the composition of the waste consists of organic waste (51.9%), plastic (20.9%), paper (9.9%), and the remaining consists of the small portion of grass, wood, metal, rubber, textile, burnable waste, and non-burnable waste.[7]

Industrial and other wastes

Industrial solid waste and other solid wastes, which include hazardous solid waste, medical solid waste, and construction and demolition waste, generate plenty of waste on the ground.

Industrial waste

Industrial solid waste refers to the solid waste that is left or generated from manufacturing activities of a factory or enterprise and that does not contain toxic or hazardous substances.[8] Four main industrial activities significantly contribute to solid waste generation, which

---

[3] R. K. Singh *et al.*, *State of Waste Management in Phnom Penh, Cambodia* (IGES Centre Collaborating with UNEP on Environmental Technologies (CCET) of Institute for Global Environmental Strategies (IGES), 2018), p. 9.

[4] *Ibid.*

[5] Provincial Departments of Planning. Data Documentation on Provincial Municipality Situation in 2015.

[6] K. Seng, *Analysis of Solid Waste Composition and Waste Forecasting in Phnom Penh with the Production of Methane from Dangkor Landfill.* Cambodia: Institute of Technology of Cambodia, 2015.

[7] *Ibid.*

[8] Ministry of Environment Cambodia. Declaration on collecting and transporting industrial solid waste in Phnom Penh, Pub. L. No. 148 (2002).

includes garment factories, brick kilns, rice milling, and rubber processing.[9]

In Phnom Penh, Sarom Trading Company is the major company that provides the service of collecting the industrial solid waste from factories such as garment factories, plastic factories, leather and paper factories to the Sarom industrial landfill located in Por Sen Chey district, Phnom Penh. Nevertheless, the Sarom industrial landfill also disposes of electronic waste, printing ink, batteries and battery waste, etc.[10] Besides the brick kilns, rice milling, and rubber processing, most of the solid wastes are disposed in the open area or openly burned.

Medical waste

Medical waste refers to the waste generated from the health care sector such as public and private hospitals, health centers, clinics, and medical laboratories.[11] Medical waste is classified into two types: (i) general waste including office residues, kitchen waste, etc. and (ii) health care waste including infectious waste (flesh, bandage, blood, etc.), sharp waste, pharmaceutical waste, chemical waste, radioactive waste, etc.[12]

As of 2011, the medical wastes are generated from eight national hospitals in Phnom Penh, 24 provincial referral hospitals, 64 district referral hospitals, 1,097 health care centers, and 87 health posts.[13] The expansion of medical services makes the quantity of waste increase

---

[9] *The Mirror*, "Environmental Pollution Has to Be Reduced in Four Industrial Target Areas," Expat Advisory Services, February 23, 2010, accessed May 18, 2015. http://www.expat-advisory.com/articles/southeast-asia/cambodia/environmental-pollution-has-be-reduced-four-industrial-target-areas.

[10] R. K. Singh *et al.*, *State of Waste Management in Phnom Penh, Cambodia* (IGES Centre Collaborating with UNEP on Environmental Technologies (CCET) of Institute for Global Environmental Strategies (IGES), 2018), p. 17.

[11] Ministry of Health. Declaration No. 19 on Waste Management from Health Care Service in the Kingdom of Cambodia (2008).

[12] Ministry of Environment (2014). Medical waste for dioxin.

[13] Project Coordination Unit (2014). Inventory report on unintentionally produced POPs in Cambodia.

rapidly. Phnom Penh generates about 40 tons per month of medical waste which comprises infectious waste, pathological waste, pharmaceutical waste, and sharps waste.[14] Most of the wastes are being dealt with by incineration, chemical treatment, and wastewater treatment.

Construction and demolition waste

Construction and demolition (C&D) waste generally includes concrete, brick, cardboard, wood, textiles, plastic, glass, metal, soil, asphalt/bitumen, insulation, and others.[15] Nevertheless, unfortunately, there is an absence of data concerning the exact amount generated from the C&D waste. The estimation can only be concluded by the types of constructed property; for instances, analyzing family resident or commercial or non-residential building according to the area of the footage. Furthermore, the condition of managing the C&D waste is very limited. Most of the mixed C&D waste which cannot be recycled is illegally dumped along the Mekong River or the open fields, since the waste is not accepted by landfill sites as an attempt to preserve the lifespan of the site; or otherwise is brought in by the contractors.[16]

Hazardous waste

Hazardous waste includes any substances which are radioactive, inflammable, infectious, oxidative, toxic, or other harmful chemical materials.[17] Further, it also consists of the waste that are generated from households, industrial and tourism sectors such as battery waste, old vehicle tires, used oil, waste from paint, agriculture pesticides, etc.

---

[14] C. Choeu, Basic Information of Medical Waste Management Unit, April 24, 2016.

[15] Royal Government of Cambodia. Sub-Decree on Garbage and Urban Solid Waste Management, Pub. L. No. 113 (2015).

[16] R. K. Singh *et al.*, *State of Waste Management in Phnom Penh, Cambodia* (IGES Centre Collaborating with UNEP on Environmental Technologies (CCET) of Institute for Global Environmental Strategies (IGES), 2018), p. 21.

[17] Royal Government of Cambodia. Sub-Decree on Garbage and Urban Solid Waste Management, Pub. L. No. 113 (2015).

Moreover, e-waste has shown a rapid increase in Phnom Penh. As the rise of usage continues, this amount is expected to grow at a high pace. The e-waste consists of items such as monitors, printers, keyboards, CPUs, typewriters, projectors, mobile phones, and PVC wires. They are collected by waste pickers and dismantlers and are sold into the market. Generally, reusable components or materials are purchased from the generators. About 3% of the residues or non-valuable components generated from dismantling, separating, and/or sorting process are disposed of, while the remaining 97% are sold to local recycling shops or transported to other recyclers on demand, or to export companies for valuable components.[18]

Methods of Waste Management in Cambodia

As a whole, the waste management or disposal is practiced differently by the government and citizens in respective areas. The disposal of waste in open spaces, along the street or into vacant areas near the residential buildings, demonstrates the lack of awareness of the citizens and the implementation of the law. Moreover, most cities and towns in the provinces have inadequate, inappropriate systems to collect, transport, and dispose of solid waste properly.

Methods of waste disposal practiced by the citizens

Cambodian people dispose of waste in various ways. Generally, there is a practice of separating recyclable or tradable solid waste at source on a voluntary basis. Waste pickers also play an important role in dividing sellable waste from waste bins and at disposal sites. For instance, there are more than 2,000 waste pickers who separate sellable waste from downtown waste bins and from the Phnom Penh landfill sites. Nevertheless, as there are no recycling plants in

[18] R. K. Singh *et al.*, *State of Waste Management in Phnom Penh, Cambodia* (IGES Centre Collaborating with UNEP on Environmental Technologies (CCET) of Institute for Global Environmental Strategies (IGES), 2018), p. 21.

Cambodia, the business of the waste pickers for sellable goods such as plastics and metals heavily depends on the export market in Vietnam.

Waste is also disposed of through burning, mostly in rural and suburban areas, as there are limited waste collection services and dumpsites. Overall, in suburban areas and rural areas, waste is being disposed of by burning (66%) or by burying near or behind houses (11%), being disposed of in rice fields, along public roads and in open spaces (9%), and in water (5%), and others (9%).[19]

Methods of waste management practiced by local authorities

The provincial, municipal authorities have contracted the tasks of collecting, transporting, and disposing of waste at landfills to private companies. The Municipality of Phnom Penh (MPP), for instance, has agreed on a 49-year contract with CINTRI (Cambodia) Ltd. to collect city waste and clean the streets since 2002. Sarom Trading Company Co. Ltd. has also been given a license by the Ministry of Environment to collect, transport, and dispose of all of Cambodia's hazardous waste at its site in Phnom Penh.

Landfill

In urban areas, wastes are managed by conventional practice with the process of collection and disposal at the dumpsite or the landfill. Approximately, about 60 dumpsites are operating across Cambodia, but the majority of them have poor quality with limited technical design.[20] Dang Kor landfill in Phnom Penh that was built in 2009 is an exception, as it has incorporated advanced techniques including compaction and a leachate drainage system. Nevertheless, this landfill

---

[19] Vanda Kham and Daniel Heilmann, *Waste Management Challenge in Cambodia and Experiences from Other Countries.* Phnom Penh: Parliamentary Institute of Cambodia, 2015, p. 3.

[20] *Ibid.*, pp. 4, 19.

also generates gas emission into the surrounding areas and the site is expected to reach its capacity by 2030.[21]

As many of the landfills are situated in flood-prone areas, it, consequently, could lead to environmental pollution. Leachate is generated during the decomposition process of the waste in the landfill, which can contaminate the groundwater table and the surrounding areas. The habitats near the landfills are exposed to health risks caused by houseflies and harmful insects. A research study concerning the habitat nearby has concluded that an increased risk of adverse health effects (e.g., low birth rate, birth defects, and certain types of cancers) has been reported near landfill sites.[22] However, since there is a lack of information on the effects of low-level environmental exposure on the general population, the risks to health from landfill sites are hard to quantify.[23]

Recycling

The local municipality has also cooperated with private companies and relevant NGOs in the field of waste management to implement composting and recycling programs. Waste composting and recycling are in operation in major cities and provinces of Cambodia. In Phnom Penh, the Phnom Penh Waste Management (PPWM) Authority in cooperation with an NGO, Cambodian Education and Waste Management Organization (COMPED), has implemented a composting project by collecting household waste in some particular areas. The PPWM is responsible for collecting organic solid waste in

---

[21] Van Vichar, "Cambodia Produces 10,000 Tons of Waste Every Day: Summit," *VOD*, September 20, 2019, accessed October 1, 2019. https://vodenglish.news/cambodia-produces-10000-tons-of-waste-every-day-summit/; See also UNDP Cambodia, "Our Plastic Problem is Out of Control. Here's How We Can Fight It," June 7, 2018, accessed November 29, 2018. http://www.kh.undp.org/content/cambodia/en/home/presscenter/articles/2018/our-plastic-problem-is-out-of-control–here-s-how-we-can-fight-i.html.

[22] M. Vrijheid, "Health Effects of Residences Near Hazardous Waste Landfill Sites: A Review of Epidemiologic Literature," *Environmental Health Perspectives* 108 (suppl 1, 2000): 101–112.

[23] *Ibid.*

particular areas (i.e., Sangkat Boeung Keng Kang I and II, and Phsar Doeum Kor Market and slaughter houses), and supplying to COMPED for the composting project.[24]

In addition, in Battambang province a composting plant is being operated close to the dumpsite. The plant is run by the COMPED with the financial support from the German Federal Ministry of Economic Cooperation and Development and the Thuringian-Cambodian Association (TKG). The composting plant receives approximately 14 tons of waste per day, of which 86.5% is likely to be organic. The plant produces a monthly output of 7 tons of compost, most of which is sold at a price of 300 riel ($0.075) per kg.[25]

Incineration

Medical waste is disposed of through incineration. Hospitals, polyclinics, clinics, and health centers that do not have their own incinerators send their waste to hospitals that have on-site facilities. Nonetheless, only small amounts of medical waste — approximately 357 kg and 68 *l* — are reported to be incinerated daily in on-site incinerators at a small number of hospitals.

Some of the ashes and residues generated from incineration are disposed of at sites in the vicinity of the incinerators, while the rest are gathered by the PSBK Company to be disposed of at open dumpsites.

Policies and Programs for Waste Management

The Royal Government of Cambodia (RGC) has established several regulations, policies, and guidelines to govern solid waste disposal in Cambodia. These regulatory documents include:

- Sub-decree on the Management of Plastic Bags (2017).
- Sub-decree on Urban Solid Waste Management (2015).

---

24 Vanda Kham and Daniel Heilmann, *Waste Management Challenge in Cambodia and Experiences from Other Countries*. Phnom Penh: Parliamentary Institute of Cambodia, 2015, p. 5.

25 *Ibid.*

- Sub-decree on Electronic Waste Management (2015).
- Sub-decree on Solid Waste Management (1999).
- The Prakas on the delegation of responsibilities to the provincial/municipality departments by implementation of the Sub-decree on the Monitoring of Water Pollution and Waste Management 2 June 1999.
- Law on the Environmental Protection and Natural Resources Management (1996).

In 2017, the Ministry of Environment has adopted a regulation on the imposition of tax on the use of plastic bags, which aims to reduce the use of plastic and change to practice of using reusable or recycle bags instead. The ministry also implemented a series of educational and awareness-raising activities on waste management for the general public.

This government also held the Clean City Contest in which 26 cities and nine districts of Phnom Penh competed on the subject of beautifying the urban areas to attract more tourists. The contest was assessed in accordance with the development of infrastructure, strengthening public services and implementing environmentally friendly initiatives. Furthermore, as part of the Clean City Program, the Ministry of Tourism and the Ministry of Environment jointly plan to set up an eco-club to promote environmental awareness and to improve the image of Cambodian cities through better management and disposal of plastic bags. The Eco-Clubs are expected to be set up at schools, universities, factories, radio, and television stations, with the engagement of the youth to further promote and educate the wider community on the benefits of clean cities.

Challenges

Concerns and issues related to waste management:

- The urban population is expanding and the generation of waste also increases rapidly. Likewise, the cost of land is increasing. More land is required for the arrangement for waste disposal and it must be located far from the residential areas. In this manner, transport length would increase so also the cost of the transportation, but the residents are still not really willing to pay. If these shortcomings continue, the standard of solid waste management in Cambodia will worsen.

- The recent expansion of some urban areas has not been planned and there is little spending on urban environment and sanitation preservation or development. Lack of solid waste disposal continues to pose a major threat to the urban environment.
- Poor waste separation at source is the main obstacle to promoting effective waste reduction and recycling activities, and such circumstances contribute to many municipal solid waste challenges, especially at final disposal sites (contributing to problems like open-pit dumping and other environmental problems due to the lack of liner, soil cover, leachate treatment, etc.).
- Environmental violations are mainly conducted outside working hours (at night) and holidays, and no systematic investigations are yet undertaken to locate the culprits.[26]
- Dumpsites in Cambodia are commonly non-compliant with traditional technical standards or guidelines; thus, there are serious risks to the environment and public health.
- Currently, there are no statutory frameworks concerning C&D waste management. C&D waste is currently included in municipal waste; however, waste producers are responsible for transporting the waste to the landfill site and are required to pay extra C&D waste disposal fees.
- Most health care providers combine medical waste with municipal waste, which is eventually collected by the Medical Waste Management Unit (MWMU).[27]
- Industrial waste disposal sites are also ineffective. Industrial solid waste and residential solid waste are often deposited together in the same dumpsite.

---

[26] C. Choeu, Basic Information of Medical Waste Management Unit, April 24, 2016.

[27] R. K. Singh *et al.*, *State of Waste Management in Phnom Penh, Cambodia* (IGES Centre Collaborating with UNEP on Environmental Technologies (CCET) of Institute for Global Environmental Strategies (IGES), 2018), p. 29.

Ways Forward

The prospect of the Cambodian Waste Management requires a strong political commitment to enhance the policies and implement the law. Some strategies are identified to address the waste management issues:

- Strengthen the position of the Municipality and MoE in waste collection, and develop municipal urban waste, liquid, and air pollution control policies.
- Perform a waste survey to determine the waste stream composition and classify the amount that can be reused and recycled. Conduct a waste survey to determine the problems of solid waste disposal caused by the unsanitary environment, which affects people. Establish community recycling waste management as a means of involving the public to increase the efficiency of solid waste management.
- In order to engage more efficiently with local communities and serve their interests, local environmental offices should be given the authority to enforce laws independently, without the requirement of the ministry's authorization.
- Basic information on waste should be made available to the public; this would be particularly useful in attracting future investment to the sector. It would be helpful to disseminate lessons learned and examples of good practice from other countries to promote information sharing and knowledge sharing.
- The government shall consider subsidy on waste management investment as that in Thailand and Vietnam.[28]
- Build alternative residential, commercial, hospital, and hazardous waste disposal sites.
- In order to recycle useful materials and resources as well as raise awareness about reducing toxic emissions through better waste management activities, e-waste recycling should be investigated.

---

[28] In Thailand, the government contributes $15 per ton of waste to processors. In Vietnam, the government contributes about $6 per ton. But we do not have anything in Cambodia.

- Efforts to increase the number of medical waste treatment facilities in line with the growth of the city should be paid attention to, realizing that people may worry about potential contamination from incineration plants.[29]
- Pilot and demonstration projects should be built to enhance e-waste management programs and procedures (e.g., waste segregation at source, separate sorting, recycling, etc.) and acquire skills and knowledge from various stakeholders in order to properly handle hazardous waste.
- Government and CINTRI should consider maintaining the current waste service fee collection scheme through EDC (electricity bill) to maintain the current income level while optimizing the differentiated weight and payment capacity-based fee system.
- Penalties should be initiated and enforced without delay for violations of waste disposal, such as open dumping of waste on fallow land, streets, rivers, etc., with transparent mechanisms to encourage the participation and support of the general public.
- Community-based solid waste management practices should be undertaken by responsible actors (i.e., local governments, community leaders, and other stakeholders concerned) starting with a focus on resolving public concerns regarding current waste management systems.
- Initiate and develop a community hotline for people to identify particular waste problems and issues (location, time, etc.) that would be resolved by the appointed authorities with concrete interventions aimed at changing behaviors, such as educating the public about waste reduction.
- Such an initiative could then be accompanied by initiatives to encourage waste separation at source when adequate recycling facilities have been developed.

[29] *Ibid.*

https://doi.org/10.1142/9789811225222_0003

Chapter 3

China–ASEAN Renewable Energy Cooperation: Practices and Policy Recommendations

Liang Dong and He Hu

China Foreign Affairs University, China

Introduction

According to the Intergovernmental Panel on Climate Change (IPCC), climate change and renewable energy demonstrate a close relationship on a global scale.[1] This scientific conclusion is also reflected in global actions. In 2015, the Paris Agreement was built upon the United Nations Framework Convention on Climate Change (UNFCCC) and brought nations to combat climate change with the long-term goals of keeping the increase in global average temperature to well below 2°C above pre-industrial levels; and limiting

[1] IPCC SR1.5, 2018. https://report.ipcc.ch/sr15/pdf/sr15_chapter4.pdf.

the increase to 1.5°C.[2] During the same year, the UN General Assembly adopted 2030 Agenda for Sustainable Development[3] and the SDG7 called to "ensure access to affordable, reliable, sustainable and modern energy for all".[4]

The process of employment on renewable energy can also provide strong support for low-carbon development, which is definitely an indispensable part of both sustainable development goals (SDGs) and the Paris Agreement on Climate Change.[5] The ASEAN–China Strategic Partnership Vision 2030 was issued in 2018, which reiterates that ASEAN and China should strengthen cooperation in environmental protection, water resources management, sustainable development, and climate change through the implementation of the ASEAN–China Strategy on Environmental Cooperation and by recognizing the importance of a regional approach in boosting clean energy development under the new ASEAN–China Clean Energy Capacity Building Program.[6] The clean energy cooperation has always played a catalytic role to foster both regional and global cooperation. However, in June 2017, the US claimed to cease all participation in the 2015 Paris Agreement on climate change, which to some extent curbs the global low-carbon development.[7] However, in April 2018,

[2] L. Dong, "Bound to Lead? Rethinking China's Role after Paris in UNFCCC Negotiations," *Chinese Journal of Population Resources and Environment* 15(1, 2017): 32–38.

[3] E. Holden, K. Linnerud and D. Banister, "The Imperatives of Sustainable Development," *Sustainable Development* 25(3, 2017): 213–226.

[4] UN, "Sustainable Development Goals: Ensure Access to Affordable, Reliable, Sustainable and Modern Energy for All," accessed May 23, 2019. https://www.un.org/sustainabledevelopment/energy/.

[5] *Xinhua News Agency*, NPC Standing Committee Approves Paris Agreement, translated November 4, 2016. http://www.xinhuanet.com/politics/2016-09/03/c_129268519.htm.

[6] ASEAN, "ASEAN–China Strategic Partnership Vision 2030," September 23, 2019. https://asean.org/asean-china-strategic-partnership-vision-2030/.

[7] N. Connor, "Beijing to Donald Trump: Climate Change is Not a Chinese Hoax," *The Telegraph*, November 17, 2016. https://www.telegraph.co.uk/news/2016/11/17/beijing-to-trump-climate-change-is-not-a-chinese-hoax/.

more than 170 nations ratified the Paris Agreement,[8] which sent a strong political signal that we are moving forward without the US.[9]

Coping with climate problems requires global efforts and wisdom.[10] In order to achieve a climate resilient future,[11] the Paris Agreement devotes to strengthening the global concerted efforts to deal with the threat of climate change by aiming to manage a global temperature rise this century to below 2°C, which means the global emissions of carbon dioxide and other major greenhouse gas (GHG) pollutants need to be reduced by more than 50% by mid-century.[12] In scientific assessment, IPCC 2014 Fifth Assessment pointed out that "CO2 emissions from fossil fuel combustion and industrial processes contributed about 78% of the total GHG emission increasing from 1970 to 2010, with a similar percentage contribution for the period 2000–2010."[13] Avoiding 2°C warming means further cuts in emissions from fossil fuel combustion. The core energy-related climate solutions[14] are those that can supply vast amounts of carbon-free energy[15] or that can use vast amounts of energy much more efficiently

---

[8] UN, "Progress of Goals 13 in 2018," accessed May 12, 2019. https://sustainabledevelopment.un.org/sdg13.

[9] M. M. Betsill, "Trump's Paris Withdrawal and the Reconfiguration of Global Climate Change Governance," *Chinese Journal of Population Resources and Environment* 15(3, 2017): 189–191.

[10] R. O. Keohane, "The International Climate Regime without American Leadership," *Chinese Journal of Population Resources and Environment* 15(3, 2017): 184–185.

[11] W. Su, "The Promoter and Builder of Global Climate Governance," *Renmin Daily*, December 1, 2015 (in Chinese).

[12] X. H. Zhang and Y. Qi, "Post-Paris Global Climate Governance: Prospects and China's Role." *China Energy* 38 (2016): 6–10 (in Chinese).

[13] IPCC, "IPCC Summery for Policymakers," accessed May 15, 2019. https://www.ipcc.ch/site/assets/uploads/2018/02/ipcc_wg3_ar5_summary-for-policymakers.pdf.

[14] F. Weiler, "Global Climate Change and Leadership: The Role of Major Players in Finding Solutions to Common Problems," *Thesais European Journal*, 2010. http://sais-journal.herokuapp.com/posts/global-climate-change-and-leadership.

[15] *Renmin Daily*, "National Unified Carbon Market to Start Soon." December 5, 2016. http://energy. people.com.cn/n1/2016/1205/c71661-28926608.html (Chinese).

in the next few decades. On the energy supply side, the core climate solutions are sustained energy, like renewable energy such as wind and solar power.

Renewable energy creates job opportunities for developing countries, especially in Asia. The size of the domestic market varies greatly from country to country, and 60% of renewable energy jobs are in Asia. Fundamentally, this data suggest that decarbonization of the global energy system can boost global economic growth and create as many as 28 million jobs in the renewable energy sector by 2050. Renewable energy creates more and more employment opportunities both in China and ASEAN (see Figure 1). In 2017, China, Europe, and the United States accounted for nearly 75% of total investment in renewable energy. In 2018, the annual report on renewable energy and employment released by the International Renewable Energy Agency (IRENA) Council shows that China, Brazil, the United States, India, Germany, and Japan remain the world's largest employers of

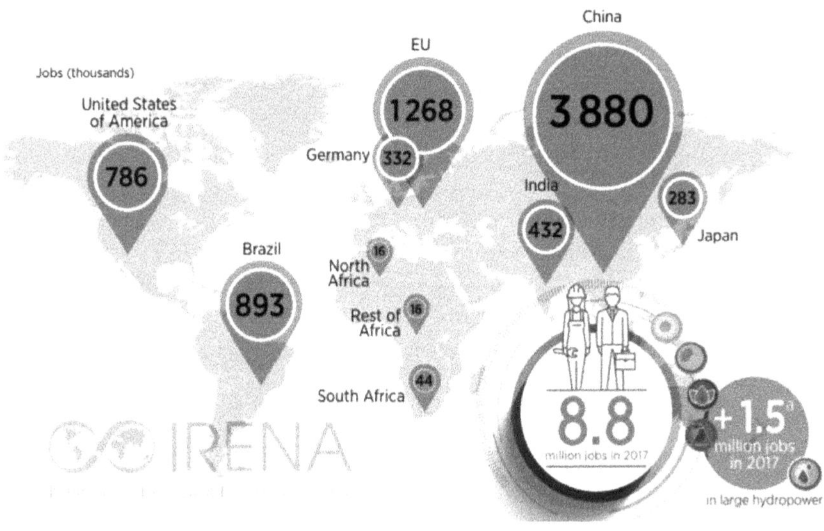

Figure 1 Renewable Energy Employment in Selected Countries

Source: IRENA, accessed May 12, 2019. https://www.irena.org/-/media/Files/IRENA/Agency/Publication/2018/May/IRENA_RE_Jobs_Annual_Review_2018.pdf.

renewable energy, accounting for more than 70% of all employment opportunities in the renewable energy industry in the world. Since 2016, China and ASEAN have continuously deepened and refined regional environmental cooperation, and reached some landmark achievements in regional cooperation in East Asia. Essentially, China and ASEAN can complement each other in terms of renewable energy, facilitating their cooperation in this area.

No country can sit on the sidelines and no country can tackle the challenge alone. Thus, China and ASEAN have shared hope for cooperation and can effectively complement each other. Although ASEAN has sufficient renewable energy, shortcomings such as capability building and lack of advanced energy equipment make it difficult to truly transform resource advantages into energy advantages. While China has accumulated experience in energy technologies such as clean coal technology, solar and wind energy, hydropower development, biomass energy, and other energy technologies. Intra-regional and even inter-regional interconnection has created new opportunities for the common development of ASEAN and China.

China and ASEAN established diverse forums and reached fruitful results on renewable energy. Minister-level forums include: ASEAN and China, Japan and South Korea Energy Ministers Meeting; East Asia Summit Energy Ministers Meeting, etc. China–ASEAN Expo and China–ASEAN Renewable Energy Forum are outstanding regional forums. The Subcommittee on Non-traditional Energy Research under the ASEAN Science and Technology Commission has cooperated with Australia, China, the European Union, Japan, India, and the United States. In 2016, the fourth China–ASEAN Technology Transfer and Innovation Cooperation Conference was held. The two sides reached an agreement on utilizing new energy and promoting the common development of national power and clean energy industries in this region. In bilateral cooperation, China Three Gorges Group and Myanmar signed the first domestic wind power project cooperation agreement, which became a landmark project of China–Myanmar energy cooperation. In 2016, China Southern Power Grid International Co., Ltd. and Vietnam signed a memorandum of cooperation on Sino-Vietnamese Xiyuan

Wind Power Project, which is the first new energy power project of a Chinese company in Vietnam.

Facts and Visions

Belt and Road Initiative (BRI) lays the foundation of cooperation between China and the ASEAN in renewable energy. Since the creation of the BRI, China has actively advanced the Green Belt and Road Partnership,[16] which will promote the cooperation in renewable energy to a new high.[17] In the Joint Communique of the Leaders Roundtable of the Belt and Road Forum for International Cooperation, it states "Enhancing cooperation in ensuring the protection of the environment,[18] of bio-diversity and of natural resources, in addressing the adverse impacts of climate change,[19] in promoting resilience and disaster-risk reduction and management, and in advancing renewable energy and energy efficiency."[20] In the list of Deliverables of the second Belt and Road Forum for International Cooperation, it stresses "We support strengthening energy infrastructure, in order to enhance energy security and to promote global access to affordable,

[16] "Greening the Belt and Road 2017," Green Finance Initiative, City of London, China Green Finance Committee, Renmin University of China, accessed March 5, 2018. http://www.gflp.org.cn/public/ueditor/php/upload/file/20181101/1541040571944776.pdf.

[17] S. Aggarwal, "The China Belt and Road Initiative Could Help or Hurt Clean Energy in Emerging Economies." 2017, accessed March 16, 2018. https://www.forbes.com/sites/energyinnovation/2017/12/04/the-china-belt-and-road-initiative-could-help-or-hurt-clean-energy-in-emerging-economies/?sh=38d15b14506e.

[18] F. Biermann and P. Pattberg, "Global Environmental Governance: Taking Stock, Moving Forward," *Annual Review Environment and Resources* 33(2008): 277–294.

[19] S. Andresen and S. Agrawala, "Leaders, Pushers and Laggards in the Making of the Climate Regime," *Global Environmental Change* 12(2002): 41–51.

[20] "Joint Communique of the Leaders Roundtable of the Belt and Road Forum for International Cooperation," Ministry of Foreign Affairs of PRC, accessed May 14, 2019. https://www.fmprc.gov.cn/mfa_eng/wjdt_665385/2649_665393/t1462012.shtml.

clean, renewable and sustainable energy for all."[21] Moreover, in the sustainable development section, it clearly reiterates that "we look forward to a climate resilient future and enhance our cooperation in areas such as environment protection,[22] circular economy, clean energy and energy efficiency, sustainable and integrated water resources management including support to the countries adversely affected by climate change,[23] in line with internationally agreed principles and obligations so as to achieve sustainable development in its three dimensions, economic, social and environmental, in a balanced and integrated manner."[24]

ASEAN also sets up its own objectives in renewable energy. ASEAN takes renewable energy cooperation as one of its priorities and has the potential to develop renewable energy on a larger scale. From the perspective of economic potential, ASEAN countries have welcomed a good opportunity to develop renewable energy. Each country sets higher goals in the proportion of renewable energy. In the "2016–2025 ASEAN Cooperative Action Plan Phase I: 2016–2020", ASEAN sets an overall regional target of 23% of renewable energy in the primary energy structure by 2025, with Laos (59%), the Philippines (41%), Indonesia (26%), Cambodia (35%), Myanmar (29%), and Thailand (24%) all having higher development goals[25] than the overall goal of ASEAN (see Figure 2).

---

[21] "Joint Communique of the Leaders' Roundtable of the Second Belt and Road Forum for International Cooperation," Ministry of Foreign Affairs of PRC, accessed May 15, 2019. https://www.fmprc.gov.cn/mfa_eng/wjdt_665385/2649_665393/t1658766.shtml.

[22] Ministry of Environment Protection of the People's Republic of China, "Guidance on Promoting 'Green Belt and Road' Construction," accessed April 6, 2017. http://www.zhb.gov.cn/gkml/hbb/bwj/201705/t20170505_413602.htm (in Chinese).

[23] R. O. Keohane and D. G. Victor, "Cooperation and Discord in Global Climate Policy," *Nature Climate Change* 6(2016): 570–575.

[24] "Joint Communique of the Leaders' Roundtable of the Second Belt and Road Forum for International Cooperation," Ministry of Foreign Affairs of PRC, accessed May 15, 2019. https://www.fmprc.gov.cn/mfa_eng/wjdt_665385/2649_665393/t1658766.shtml.

[25] M. G. D. Stafford-Smith, O. Gaffney, F. Ullah, B. Reyers, N. Kanie, B. Stigson, P. Shrivastava, M. Leach, D. O'Connell, "Integration: The Key to Implementing the Sustainable Development Goals," *Sustainability Science* 12(6, 2016): 911–919.

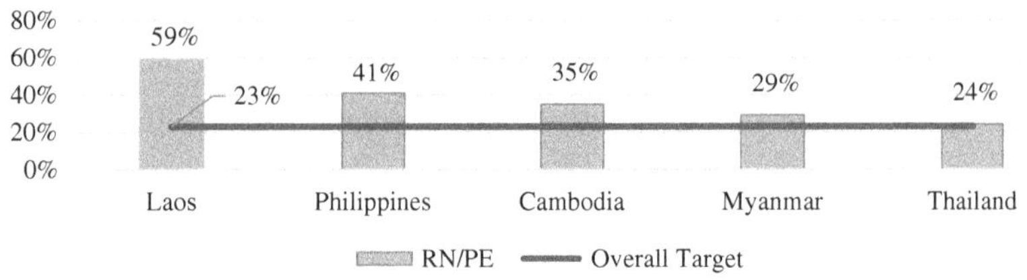

Figure 2 Renewable Energy in the Primary Energy Structure by 2025

Both China and ASEAN recognize the importance of a regional approach in boosting clean energy development. In order to realize connectivity among the ASEAN countries, in 1997, the leaders of ASEAN countries proposed the "ASEAN Power Grid" initiative at the Second ASEAN Informal Summit. In 2007, the energy ministers signed a memorandum of understanding on the objectives, obligations, and implementation of the ASEAN Power Grid. In the "ASEAN Energy Cooperation Action Plan (2016–2025)", it is proposed to gradually form regional interconnection at bilateral, subregional and ASEAN levels, and realize the vision of all-round comprehensive cooperation of regional energy and power. In the 33rd ASEAN Ministers on Energy Meeting, ministers emphasized that it is important to advance clean energy development in ASEAN, including renewable energy, energy efficiency, and clean technology applications.[26] In the document of Plan of Action to Implement the Joint Declaration on ASEAN–China Strategic Partnership for Peace and Prosperity, enhancing energy cooperation[27] and encouraging investment in joint energy infrastructure of renewable and alternative energy together with information sharing and technical exchange in the development of new and renewable energy sources and technologies were reiterated. Forging ahead, based on the ASEAN–China

[26] "Joint Ministerial Statement of the Thirty Third ASEAN Ministers on Energy Meeting (33rd AMEM)," ASEAN, accessed May 12, 2019. https://asean.org/joint-ministerial-statement-the-thirty-third-asean-ministers-on-energy-meeting/.

[27] P. M. Haas, "Addressing the Global Governance Deficit," *Global Environmental Politics* 4(4, 2004): 1–15.

Strategic Partnership Vision 2030,[28] two parties will implement active cooperation under the new ASEAN–China Clean Energy Capacity Building Program.[29]

China's Low Carbon Development: The Trends and Policies

China's energy consumption is facing a crucial transition. The total consumption of fossil energy in China will peak in 2020 and decline steadily before 2035. The proportion of coal in the power generation and industrial sectors continues to shrink. The level of electrification in the industrial and transportation sectors has risen significantly, slowing China's dependence on oil imports. If the future renewable energy economy fully catches up with fossil energy, China does not need to use natural gas as a transitional energy source between coal and renewable energy. At national level, with energy cooperation movement and institutionalization, China aims at building a "clean, low-carbon, safe and efficient" modern energy system.[30] It depends on the feasible path and necessary steps for the transformation of China's energy system from fossil energy to renewable energy. To promote renewable energy, China has accelerated the implementation of Ecological Civilization and has made notable progress in implementing a package of domestic reforming measures on Ecological Civilization Construction System. The 19th National Congress of the Communist Party of China raised the construction of ecological civilization to a new height and regarded it as one of the goals to be

---

[28] J. P. Xi, "Work Together to Implement 2030 Agenda for Sustainable Development," *Xinhuanet*, accessed September 5, 2017. http://www.xinhuanet.com/world/2017-09/05/c_129696447.htm.

[29] ASEAN, "ASEAN–China Strategic Partnership Vision 2030," accessed May 12, 2019, https://asean.org/asean-china-strategic-partnership-vision-2030/.

[30] Z. H. Xie, "Promotion of Green Low-Carbon Development and Participation in Global Climate Governance," *China Economic Trade Guide* 4 (2016): 59 (translated from Chinese).

achieved by 2050.[31] The realization of this goal requires strong institutional guarantees which show that the reform of the power system needs to ensure the existing market players' role as the main force.[32] China must fully implement the overall plan for promoting economic, political, cultural, social, and ecological progress to ensure coordinated progress in all areas of modernization, so as to balance the relations of production with the productive forces as well as the superstructure with the economic base, and continue to expand the path of development that leads to increased production, prosperity, and a good ecosystem.[33]

In July 2018, the National Development and Reform Commission and the National Energy Administration issued the "Energy Technology Revolution Innovation Action Plan (2016–2030)," and at the same time released the "Energy Technology Revolution Key Innovation Action Roadmap." In the field of renewable energy, China focuses on developing higher efficiency, lower cost, more flexible wind energy, solar energy technology, biomass energy, geothermal energy, ocean energy utilization technology, renewable hydrogen energy production, and heating technology.

On departmental and ministerial levels, different institutions devote to improving the coordination and cooperation mechanism between government departments. China's mitigation route design is closely related to the goal of ecological civilization and sustainable energy systems. Thanks to the deepening of re-electrification, overall emissions from the power generation and heating sectors could be significantly reduced due to energy technology upgrading in the near future. According to the latest China Renewable Development Report 2018 released by National Energy Administration, China's

[31] CPC 2018, "Report of the 19th CPC Congress," accessed October 18, 2017. http://www. xinhuanet.com/politics/19cpcnc/2017-10/18/c_1121822489.htm (in Chinese).

[32] *Xinhua News Agency*, " An Introduction to the Report of 19th CPC National Congress," accessed October 18, 2017. http:// www.xinhuanet.com/ politics/19cpcnc/2017-10/18/c_11218 22489.htm (in Chinese).

[33] Report at 18th Party Congress, accessed July 07, 2019. http://language. chinadaily.com.cn/news/2012-11/19/content_15941774_2.htm.

clean and renewable energy continues to grow. The construction process of a clean, low-carbon, safe, and efficient energy system is actively accelerating to promote the green development of energy, which constitutes an important part of the construction of ecological civilization, and the energy development in the new era.[34]

On a provincial level, local governments are also likely to promote renewable energy to further enhance their enthusiasm and initiatives in energy transformation as well as the role of government leadership[35] and supervision. Provinces take proactive approaches in international cooperation on renewable energy. For instance, in 2009, China–ASEAN New Energy and Renewable Energy Development and Utilization International Science and Technology Cooperation Forum was successfully held in Yunnan Province. The year of 2018 marks the 10th anniversary of Eco Forum Global Annual Conference, which was held for 10 consecutive years in Guizhou Province. In President Xi Jinping's Congratulatory Letter to the 2018 Annual Conference, he expressed that China would stick to the path of green and sustainable development. China is ready to work with the international community to realize the 2030 Agenda for Sustainable Development and build a clean, beautiful world.[36] In 2017, the third East Asia Summit Clean Energy Forum was held in Kunming, Yunnan Province, which is another important institution on renewable energy pushing green development and energy transition toward a cleaner future.

With the involvement of central and local governments, international cooperation on renewable energy has been actively promoted. Central government has deepened the international cooperation and exchange of energy science and technology. China formulates an

---

[34] *Renmin Daily*, accessed July, 09 2019. http://energy.people.com.cn/n1/2019/0627/c71896-31199589.html.

[35] B. Conrad, "China in Copenhagen: Reconciling the Beijing Climate Revolution and the Copenhagen Climate Obstinacy," *The China Quarterly* 210(2012): 435–455.

[36] A. Steiner, "The Extraordinary Opportunity of the 2030 Agenda for Sustainable Development," *The European Journal of Development Research* 30(2, 2018): 163–165.

international strategy for energy technology innovation[37] and actively carries out all-round, multi-level, and high-end international cooperation in energy technology. China also leverages international and domestic energy technology resources, actively integrates into the global innovation network[38] and enhances China's ability in the strategic resource allocation of global energy technology. In international cooperation and exchanges, relevant departments pay attention to building communication and dialogue platforms for enterprises in terms of technical cooperation, intellectual property rights, and cross-border mergers and acquisitions. The government has encouraged energy companies, universities, and research institutions to carry out joint technological innovations with relevant foreign institutions.

Renewable energy cooperation unleashes unlimited potential under the BRI framework. In conjunction with the implementation of the BRI, China relies on major energy projects to promote China's advanced energy technologies, equipment and standards of "going out".[39] The development potential of renewable energy in the countries along the BRI is tremendous.[40] Chinese government and enterprises should give full play to their advantages in new energy manufacturing, project design, and construction and actively help countries along the route to develop renewable energy. Promoting the development of renewable energy will not only help to reduce the adverse effects of climate change to protect the environment and the health of the people, to accelerate the transformation of energy

---

[37] N. Kanie and F. Biermann, *Governing through Goals: Sustainable Development Goals as Governance Innovation*. Cambridge, MA: MIT Press, 2017.

[38] H. Bulkeley, "Reconfiguring Environmental Governance: Towards a Politics of Scales and Networks," *Political Geography* 24(8, 2005): 875–902.

[39] UNEP, "A Green Belt and Road," accessed March 7, 2018. https://www.unenvironment.org/news-and-stories/press-release/green-belt-and-road.

[40] S. M. Qian, "China's Permanent Representative to the United Nations: 'The Belt and Road' Promotes the Realization of 2030 Agenda for Sustainable Goals," *CRI Online*, accessed April 12, 2017. http://news.cri.cn/20170412/66933d9a-6e26-ee23-7c2d-9ab15fab2328.html.

structure, but also help China create a good international image of the BRI.[41]

China–ASEAN Renewable Energy Cooperation Mechanisms and Cooperative Recommendations

Regional cooperation in energy sector should be strengthened to build a more sustainable energy system. It requires countries to actively carry out all-round, multi-level, and high-level international cooperation in energy technology innovation as well as focus on some field cooperation, such as technology and equipment cooperation, and human resource exchanges. In order to make full use of international and domestic energy technology resources to actively integrate into the global innovation network and to enhance China's ability in the strategic resource allocation of global energy technology, recommendations are as follows:

China–ASEAN should boost their renewable energy cooperation at regional level. ASEAN has the potential to develop renewable energy on a larger scale. For instance, Indonesia has the most abundant renewable energy resources with various types. The water, geothermal, and biomass resources rank first in ASEAN, and geothermal resources account for 40% of the total global geothermal resources. Wind resources are mainly concentrated in Vietnam, Laos, Thailand, and some coastal areas, of which Vietnam is the most abundant. The solar resources of ASEAN countries are also very rich. However, with shortcomings such as capability building and lack of advanced energy equipment, it is hard to truly transform resource advantages into energy advantages. To complement ASEAN, China has accumulated experience in energy technology such as clean coal technology, solar and wind energy, hydropower development, biomass energy, and other energy technologies.

---

[41] L. Dong, "Bound to Lead? Rethinking China's Role after Paris in UNFCCC Negotiations," *Chinese Journal of Population Resources and Environment* 15(1, 2017): 32–38.

Therefore, from the perspective of potential, China and ASEAN countries embrace a good opportunity to develop renewable energy together.

China should synergize renewable energy cooperation under the BRI framework with ASEAN–China Strategic-Partnership Vision 2030. With China's BRI, the development potential of renewable energy in the countries along the "Belt and Road" is huge. The Chinese government and enterprises should give full play to their advantages in new energy manufacturing, project design and construction, and actively help countries along the route to develop renewable energy. China's "BRI" renewable energy cooperation still has many opportunities. The main obstacles include excessive project financing costs, low international recognition of Chinese standards, insufficient support for renewable energy in countries along the route, and related legal and policy risks. Therefore, promoting the development of renewable energy will not only help reduce the adverse effects of climate change, protect the environment and the health of the people, and accelerate the transformation of energy structure but also help China to create a good international image of BRI. In the List of Deliverables of the first Belt and Road Forum for International Cooperation, the relevant departments of the Chinese government issued the following documents: Building the Belt and Road: Concept, Practice and China's Contribution, and Vision and Actions on Promoting Energy Cooperation on the Belt and Road. In the Joint Communique of the Leaders Roundtable of the Belt and Road Forum for International Cooperation, Article Six emphasizes the opportunities that can be created by communication and coordination among other global, regional and national frameworks and initiatives for promoting cooperation in connectivity and sustainable development, such as 2030 Agenda for Sustainable Development, ASEAN Community Vision 2025, and Master Plan on ASEAN Connectivity 2025.[42]

[42] Joint Communique of the Leaders Roundtable of the Belt and Road Forum for International Cooperation, accessed July 8, 2019. https://www.en84.com/fy/fwx/xy/2757.html.

In the List of Deliverables of the second Belt and Road Forum for International Cooperation, nine energy cooperation projects have been listed. ASEAN countries have established energy cooperation partnership with China. China Investment Corporation will bring financial input to renewable energy cooperation projects in Asia-Pacific.

At national level, China will still adhere to bilateral cooperation. In the past five years, China has established 56 bilateral energy cooperation mechanisms with relevant countries and participated in 29 multilateral energy cooperation mechanisms, and signed more than 100 cooperation agreements.

In the international cooperation and exchanges, relevant departments pay attention to building communication and dialogue platforms for enterprises in terms of technical cooperation, intellectual property rights and cross-border mergers and acquisitions, and encourage energy companies, universities, and research institutions to carry out joint technological innovations with relevant foreign institutions.

At the provincial level, it is encouraged to have provincial and local renewable energy cooperation. For instance, the climate conditions in Guangxi and ASEAN are similar with the same tropical and subtropical climates. Except for Singapore and Brunei, ASEAN countries, like China, generally use fuelwood and straw as the mainstay. Renewable energy technologies and management models developed and promoted by Guangxi and other places in China to promote the sustainable development of the rural economy can also be transplanted in ASEAN countries and can be widely applied through appropriate technological improvements. Biogas and comprehensive utilization of technology represent the most projects covering renewable energy in Guangxi and ASEAN countries. Yunnan has solar energy cooperation with ASEAN countries. Gansu is one of China's energy resource gathering places. It has abundant wind resources and sufficient solar energy resources.[43] It is a good place to develop new energy sources such as wind power and photovoltaic.

[43] M. Zürn and B. Faude, "On Fragmentation, Differentiation, and Coordination," *Global Environmental Politics* 13(3, 2013): 119–130.

China and ASEAN should enhance technology and equipment cooperation. In terms of technical cooperation, the two sides can promote exchanges and cooperation in technology, management, and other aspects, promote the advanced technology standards, jointly promote the progress of clean energy technology, and reduce costs. In power supply construction, the two sides can jointly further build a number of clean energy projects such as hydropower, wind power, solar power generation, and stations for power storage to jointly promote the scale development of renewable energy and improve the level of capacity building.

By developing interconnection and interoperability, the two sides can strengthen joint research on regional power grid cooperation, and promote the interconnection of power grids in ASEAN. As for industrial cooperation, the two sides can further expand cooperation areas by strengthening information sharing such as policies, plans, and projects, extend the industrial chain for energy and electric power cooperation, and promote the ASEAN industrial upgrading.

China and ASEAN will advance human resources exchange. All sides should continuously implement the human resources exchange project. Take the China–Laos Joint Laboratory for Renewable Energy for instance. On 24 August 2018, the China–Laos Joint Laboratory for Renewable Energy Development and Utilization passed the test of the Ministry of Science and Technology of China in Kunming, Yunnan Province. It is cofounded by the Institute of Renewable Energy and New Materials of Yunnan Normal University and Laos Ministry of Science and Technology in 2013. In September, they were jointly set up to provide Laos with renewable energy experimental demonstration technology and equipment, help to cultivate professional talents, jointly develop and utilize renewable energy, and implement the BRI and the "China–ASEAN Technology Partner Program."

During the implementation of the project, both parties have established joint laboratories including solar photovoltaic utilization and new materials laboratory, solar thermal utilization laboratory, bioenergy comprehensive development and utilization laboratory, and solar energy utilization quality testing center in Laos. China has donated more than 1,000 sets of experimental instruments and equipment such as solar photovoltaic, photothermal and biomass energy equipment to Laos, and has built 20 demonstration sites for renewable energy in Laos.

Conclusion

Renewable energy cooperation between China and ASEAN will not only promote future renewable energy innovation development among countries but also bring concrete and tangible benefits to their people. With the endogenous drive and exogenous joint efforts, it is justified to say that renewable energy cooperation will be one of the pilot cooperation fields and the most efficient cooperation modes for the future development. It is believed that with deepening cooperation on renewable energy, China and ASEAN can enhance their trust and take it to a new height. Although there are many challenges, such as financial, technological, and market-related barriers, China and ASEAN will take great effort to achieve affordability, sustainability, and reliability in energy supply in renewable energy cooperation, and accomplish regional peace, stability, prosperity, and harmony. As a community with a shared future, China and ASEAN will synergize 2030 Agenda for Sustainable Development[44] and Strategy 2025 to fully realize their potential on renewable energy.[45]

---

[44] UN, "Transforming Our World: The 2030 Agenda for Sustainable Development," accessed March 7, 2018. https://sustainabledevelopment.un.org/content/documents/21252030%20Agenda%20for%20Sustainable%20Development%20web.pdf.

[45] L. Dong and H. B. Zhang, "Environmental Objectives in 2030 SDGS and Its Implications on the World and China in Environmental Governance," *Chinese Journal of Population Resources and Environment* 26 (2016): 8–15 (translated from Chinese).

https://doi.org/10.1142/9789811225222_0004

Chapter

4

China's Environmental Protection in the New Era from the Perspective of Eco-Civilization Construction

Qingzhi Huan

Peking University, China

Introduction

Owing to the arduous efforts of academia and the continuous promotion from practice over the past decade of 2008–2018, "eco-civilization" (*shengtai wenming*) or "eco-civilization construction" (*shengtai wenming jianshe*) in the context of contemporary China has largely established its status both as a policy system and an academic discourse,[1] though there are still some difficulties or obstacles to

[1] Qingzhi Huan, "The Basic Concepts Concerning Eco-Civilization and Its Theories," *Study with Socialism with Chinese Characteristics,* 4(2018a): 16–26; Qingzhi Huan, "The Triple Visions of Elaborating the Socialist Outlook on Eco-civilization," *Journal of Beijing Administrative Institute,* 4(2018b): 63–70; Qingzhi Huan, "Construction of the Eco-Civilization Demonstration Areas from a

make it internationally heard and recognized.[2] As the core concept of an academic discourse, eco-civilization or eco-civilization construction is widely defined as an ecological negation and transcendence of modern industrial and urban civilization; thus, closely connecting with a new pattern of economic, social, and cultural institutional framework as well as its corresponding perception basis. In other words, eco-civilization will definitely be a new civilization based on a new science of ecology rather than modern science and

---

Three-Dimensional Perspective: Evaluation and Prospect," *Journal of China University of Geosciences*, 3(2017a): 54–63; Shinan Fang. *A Study of Marx's Environmental Thoughts and the Environment Friendly Society*. Shanghai: Sanlian Publishing House, 2014; Qingzhi Huan, Li Hongwei and Lin Zhen, *Ten Lectures on Eco-civilization Construction*. Beijing: The Commercial Press, 2014; Sihua Liu, *The Eco-Marxist Basic Principles of Economics*. Beijing: People's Press, 2014/2006; Yunfei Zhang, *Eco-civilization from a Perspective of Historical Materialism*. Beijing: Renmin University of China Press, 2014, Feng Lu, *New Thoughts on Eco-Civilization*. Beijing: China Science and Technology Press, 2013; Mingchu Wang and Yang Yingzi, *Theory and Practice of Socialist Eco-civilization Construction*. Beijing: People's Press, 2011; Mouchang Yu, *On Eco-civilization*. Beijing: Central Compilation and Translation Press, 2010; Xueming Chen. *On Eco-Civilization*. Chongqing: Chongqing Press, 2008; Fengzhang Wu, *Eco-civilization Construction: Theory and Practice*. Beijing: Central Compilation and Translation Press, 2008; Zhenhai Ji (ed.), *On Eco-Civilization*. Beijing: People's Press, 2007.

[2] Elizabeth Lord, *Building an Ecological Civilization across the Rural/Urban Divide and the Politics of Environmental Knowledge Production in Contemporary China*. Toronto: University of Toronto, 2018; Maurizio Marinelli, "How to Build a 'Beautiful China' in the Anthropocene: The Political Discourse and the Intellectual Debate on Ecological Civilization," *Journal of Chinese Political Science* (2018). https://doi.org/10.1007/s11366-018-9538-7; Arran Gare, *The Philosophical Foundations of Ecological Civilization: A Manifesto for the Future*. London: Routledge Environmental Humanities, 2016; Qingzhi Huan, "Socialist Eco-Civilization and Social-Ecological Transformation," *Capitalism Nature Socialism* 27/2(2016a): 51–66; Fred Magdoff, "Harmony and Ecological Civilization: Beyond the Capitalist Alienation of Nature," *Monthly Review* 64/2(2012): 1–9; Fred Magdoff, "Ecological Civilization," *Monthly Review*, 62/8(2011): 1–25; Ariel Salleh, "Eco-Socialism and 'Ecological Civilization' in China," *Capitalism Nature Socialism*, 19/3(2008): 122–128; Roy Morrison, "Building an Ecological Civilization," *Social Anarchism: A Journal of Theory and Practice*, 38(2007): 1–18.

technology.[3] And as an emerging systematic theory of environmental politics and ecological culture, eco-civilization or eco-civilization construction can be expounded from three aspects or sub-dimensions.[4] Namely, it is a "green-left" ideological discourse on development of the governing political party (Communist Party of China, henceforth CPC), an environmental political–social theory insisting on a comprehensive transformation or re-construction of the contemporary society, and an organic way of thinking and a philosophy with a strong link to the Chinese and/or Western Classical tradition.

Arguably, there are two inseparable levels or dimensions with the eco-civilization construction of China in the New Era after the 18th National Congress of CPC which was held in 2012.[5] On the one hand, governments at all levels as well as the whole society should firmly establish and consciously carry out "the socialist outlook on eco-civilization" expounded clearly at the 19th National Congress of CPC in 2017,[6] or to put it differently, lead or regulate the process of eco-civilization construction in China with a "new socialist politics".[7]

---

[3] Feng Lu, *New Thoughts on Eco-civilization*. Beijing: China Science and Technology Press, 2013.

[4] Qingzhi Huan,"The Eco-Civilization Theory and Its Implications for Green Change," *Marxism & Realities,* 5(2015): 167–175.

[5] As for the accurate starting-point of New Era, a common understanding is the 18th National Congress of CPC in November 2012, at which Xi Jinping was elected as the top leader of CPC, though this term was first used in the working report to 19th National Congress of CPC in October 2017.

[6] In the work report to the 18th National Congress of CPC in 2012, the accurate expression is "Striving for a new era of socialist eco-civilization". Of course, even after the 19th National Congress of CPC in 2017, the accuracy implications of "socialist outlook on eco-civilization" or "socialist eco-civilization" is still a controversial or even a deliberately avoided issue (Jinping Xi, *The Working Report to the 19th Congress of CPC.* Beijing: People's Press, 2017a; Jinping Xi, *The Working Report to the 18th Congress of CPC.* Beijing: People's Press, 2012; Qingzhi Huan, "The Triple Visions of Elaborating the Socialist Outlook on Eco-civilization," *Journal of Beijing Administrative Institute,* 4(2018b): 63–70; Qingzhi Huan, "Socialist Eco-Civilization and Social-Ecological Transformation," *Capitalism Nature Socialism,* 27/2(2016a): 51–66.

[7] Qingzhi Huan, "New Political Vision 2.0 of Eco-Civilization," *People's Tribune,* October 2014: 38–41.

On the other hand, more concrete policy initiatives or public policy instruments of environmental economy and environmental public administration should be introduced and applied to push forward as soon as possible the modernization of China's ecological environmental governance system and governance capacity. In such a specific context, an interesting question is to what extent can the discourse of socialist eco-civilization and its practice in China reshape or change the relationship among eco-capital, green technology, and public participation in reality?

Two Clues of Theoretical Analysis

Theoretically, there are at least two clues to be followed in analyzing the issue aforementioned. The first clue is the interaction among eco-capital, green technology, and public participation. It should be noted that "eco-capital" here mainly refers to certain new forms and scopes of natural ecosystem and its components that become economic resources and/or capitals, rather than those industrial and commercial natural resources and/or capitals in the traditional sense which are closely related to the exploitation, transportation, and processing of natural resources.[8] Not only that, a more significant difference between "eco-capital" and traditional industrial and commercial natural capitals is that the former is to a certain degree based on our recognition of independent or unique value of natural eco-system and its elements. For instance, it should first of all include the economic value of repair (replacement) once one natural eco-system and its elements are contaminated or damaged. Thus, "eco-capital" targets at a

[8] Qiang Li, "Public Participation in the Process of Capital Ecologicalization: Taking Fuzhou City as an Example," *Journal of Poyang Lake,* 5(2018): 52–57; Xiaomin Wei and Yang Li, "Making the Eco-Capital to be Flowing 'Invaluable Asset'," *Xinhua Daily*, December 4, 2018; Wenhu Ye, "Harmonious Co-existence between Human and Nature Depends on the Development of Green Capital," *Economic Information Daily*, August 17, 2015; Hong Yin, "Protecting Natural Ecological Capital with the Professional Thinking and Manner," *Journal of the Chinese People's Political Consultative Conference*, November 12, 2015.

better use and protection of natural eco-system and its elements. Similarly, the term "green technology" does not cover all the technological processes and means that are invented to deal with the natural eco-system and its elements. Rather, it mainly refers to the technological processes and means that are more environmentally friendly than traditional ones until their negative impacts on nature are zero.[9] Thus, just like the case of "eco-capital", "green technology" is also strongly relative or hierarchical. For example, we can distinguish them into different categories such as "light green" or "dark green" "eco-capital" and "light green" or "dark green" "green technology". As for "public participation", although it is supposed to include the participation of capital owners (such as state, communities and private capitalists) and research and development personnel (organizational units and individuals), here it more often than not refers to economic, social and political participation or involvements of the common people, directly or indirectly connected with the introduction and application of "eco-capital" and "green technology".[10]

Such a conceptual interpretation aforementioned is very important for us to correctly understand the relationship among eco-capital, green technology, and public participation in the process of socialist eco-civilization construction of China. On the one hand, both eco-capital and green technology may to varying degrees affect production and public life of various sizes of societies (communities), and accordingly, they need to be examined and controlled democratically by the public who are affected and/or related. In other words, the specific forms of eco-capital and green technology are also parts of the production and life of the entire society, especially those concrete

[9] Jin Guo, "Further Improving the Jiangsu's Innovation Level of Green Technology." *Xinhua Daily*, 19 February 2019; Fating Yang, *An Institutional Study on the Innovation of Green Technology: From a Perspective of Eco-Civilization*. Beijing: Party School of CPC Central Committee, 2014.

[10] Lingyan Hu, *A Study on the Public Participation in Eco-civilization Construction of Contemporary China*. Quanzhou: Huaqiao University, 2016; Shengxun Shi and Chen Aili, "On Public Participation in Eco-Civilization of China," *Economy of Forestry*, 3(2016): 25–29; Yue Wang, *A Study on Public Participation in Eco-civilization Construction of China*. Dalian: Dalian University of Technology, 2015.

eco-capitals and green technologies associated with the field of mass consumption. On the other hand, the policy decision-making or choice capacity of the public for eco-capital and green technology is a significant indicator to test the eco-civilization level of Chinese society, and this is especially true for the characteristics of socialist eco-civilization. In other words, a more authentic or higher degree of socialist eco-civilization means that the society as a whole will be more inclined to encourage the "red-green" versions of "eco-capital" and "green technology", consciously combining the orientation of ecological protection and the consideration of social justice.

What can be drawn from aforesaid analysis is that, different from the critical viewpoints of many eco-Marxists on eco-capital and green technology,[11] there may be a positive possibility in reality. That is to say, the creative introduction and application of eco-capital and green technology can act as a player promoting public participation or involvement in the process of eco-civilization construction of China, especially considering its socialist institutional framework. The implicit logical mechanism can be summarized as follows. Democratic decision-making of governments at different levels and supervision action of the participatory public, directly (acting as the production operators and consumers) or indirectly (acting as the social members or citizens) can to a great degree determine the selection of pattern, application scope and consequence response of eco-capital and green technology, which will turn out to be the motivating reasons or social conditions to further encourage and promote the public participation or involvement.

The second analytical clue which can be followed is the interactive relationship among eco-capital, cultural capital, and industrial capital. In my opinion, the term "Green development" in the discursive context of contemporary China,[12] from the perspective of

[11] Victor Wallis, *Red-Green Revolution: The Politics and Technology of Eco-Socialism*. Toronto: Political Animal Press, 2018.

[12] Jiahua Pan, "From Ecological Imbalance to Eco-Civilization: A Transformative Process of Green Development over 40 Years of Reform and Opening-Up," *Urban and Environmental Studies*, 4(2019): 3–16; Jiancheng Chen *et al.*, *Promoting Green Development and Realizing a Well-off Society in an All-round Way*. Beijing: China Forestry Press, 2018.

environmental economics or resource management, can be generalized as a proper disposal with the relationship among eco-capital, cultural capital, and industrial capital. "Green development" is an umbrella term with quite broad implications and different usages. In most cases, it can be regarded as the synonym for sustainable development or environmentally friendly development in a general sense. Thus, it represents a certain degree of "greening" of the development discourse which has thus far had a much longer history, resulting in a less harmful ecological and environmental damage in the process of economic and social modernization development. Even in the discursive context of eco-civilization construction, there are at least three slightly different expressions for "Green development". They are "Three developments" (*san ge fazhan*), "Five new development concepts" (*wu ge xin fazhan linian*) and "Strategies(approaches) of eco-civilization construction" (*shengtai wenming jianshe zhanlue/lujing*).[13] "Three developments" include "green development" "low carbon development", and "circular development" side by side, mainly emphasizing the green or environment-friendly characteristics of economic and/or industry(products) structure, while the latter two developments more refer to the features of low- (GC) (adfective) carbon emissions and the closed recycling of raw materials in the economic production process. Rather, what "Green development" as one of the "Five new development concepts" stresses is that consideration of eco-civilization or environmental friendliness has become the guiding principle for China's socialist modernization, from overall planning to concrete practice, just like the roles of other four new development concepts of innovation, coordination, openness, and sharing. By contrast, "Green development" as a strategy or practical approach of eco-civilization construction highlights the importance of improving China's eco-civilization construction level through gradually building a green industrial and economic system, green energy supply system, green technical support system, and green living consumption system. For the purpose of writing this chapter, the

---

[13] Qingzhi Huan, "The Evolution of CPC's Green Modernization Discourse since 40-Year Reform and Opening Up," *The Journal of Yunmen*, 1(2019): 14–24.

concept of "Green development" is mainly used in the third sense. More concretely, for improving the level of eco-civilization construction in China through the greening of economic system, energy system, technologic system and living and consumption styles, in the capital management point of view, there are at least two different approaches or tactics. They are either by utilizing the relatively strong industrial capital to support and cultivate eco-capital and cultural capital, or by taking advantages of the relatively rich ecological and cultural capitals to attract and accumulate industrial capital. For the former, I call it the "Eco-modernization path", with Jiangsu Province and Guangdong Province as the actual examples; and for the latter, it is called "Green development path", with Jiangxi Province[14] and Fujian Province[15] as the typical examples.

From the standpoint of eco-civilization and its construction, on the one hand, a higher or more fundamental objective for introducing eco-capital and cultural capital is to realize a more effective protection of natural ecosystems and cultural heritages. Although the exploitation and utilization of natural ecosystems and cultural and historical heritages as a specific resource should not be questioned or even denied, the top issue to be targeted at by introducing eco-capital and cultural capital is that they should be better protected and inherited in the ongoing process of modernization. In this regard, eco-capital and cultural capital have an obvious feature of virtual or instrumental capital, which cannot be simply regarded as industrial and commercial capital in the traditional sense, especially those forms shaped in the context of capitalist institutional relations and discourse.[16] On the other hand, at least as far as the primary stage of socialism in China is concerned, the active role of traditional industrial and commercial

[14] Qingzhi Huan, "The Green Development Path for Eco-Civilization Construction: A Case of Jiangxi Province," *Journal of Poyang Lake*, 1(2017b): 29–41.

[15] Qingzhi Huan, "The Eco-Modernization Path for Eco-Civilization Demonstration Province Construction," *Yuejiang Academic Journal*, 8/6(2016b): 23–35.

[16] Ulrich Brand and Markus Wissen, "The Financialization of Nature as Crisis Strategy," *Journal für Entwicklungspolitik*, 30/2(2014): 16–45; Paul Hawken, Amory Lovins and L. Hunter Lovins, *Natural Capitalism: Creating the Next Industrial Revolution*. New York: Little, Brown and Company, 1999.

capital cannot be simply negated, especially for those larger-scale administrative divisions or social communities.[17] A notable question in this regard is how to gradually weaken or replace the dominant economic evaluation standards/systems and improve the existing performance evaluation standards/systems of eco-civilization construction, such as the "Green development index" evaluation system formulated by National Bureau of Statistics and National Development and Reform Commission (NDRC).[18] Arguably, current official evaluation systems of eco-civilization construction are still biased toward exploitation, utilization, and social allocation of natural resources rather than based on the protection and restoration of natural ecosystems.[19]

Generally speaking, "Green development approach (strategy)" in a narrow sense is the most common model of eco-civilization construction in China today, especially in the various forms of demonstration zones, pioneer demonstration zones, and pilot areas, trying to get started the dynamic process of eco-civilization construction with its relative rich eco-capital and/or cultural capital, for instance, the cases of Anji County, Zhejiang Province,[20] and Kang County, Gansu Province.[21] And admittedly, for those administrative jurisdictions or territories higher than county level, how to deal with traditional industrial and commercial capital is still a controversial and very difficult issue. At present, what we can safely say is that the political

---

[17] Jinping Xi, *Discussion Excerpts on Socialist Eco-civilization Construction*. Beijing: Central Party Literature Press, 2017b.

[18] According to the national evaluation results bulletin of 2016 which was released in December 2017, the most developed municipals or provinces such as Beijing, Fujian, Zhejiang, Shanghai, and Chongqing came out in front.

[19] Geng Yan *et al.*, *Annual Report on China's Provincial Eco-civilization Index*. Beijing: Social Science Academic Press, 2010–2016; Xin Qi, "A Study of the Eco-Civilization Construction Evaluation Index System," *Ecological Economy*, 12(2013): 182–186.

[20] Qingzhi Huan, "The Regional Model of Eco-Civilization Construction: A Case of Anji County," *Journal of Guizhou Provincial Party School*, 4(2016c): 32–39.

[21] Qingzhi Huan, "Ecological Industrialization, Beautiful Countryside and Eco-Civilization Construction," *China Ecological Civilization*, 4(2015b): 64–68.

ideology of "socialist outlook on eco-civilization" and the national strategy of vigorously promoting eco-civilization construction of contemporary China have created a quite favorable societal environment, within which at least certain local pioneering areas can try and successfully achieve a relative balance and internal consistency of the three types of capitals in reality (especially reflected in their industrial structure). Moreover, it seems that those administrative or geographic areas excessively concentrated with the traditional manufacturing industries and the related industries are confronting more difficulties and obstacles to starting such a green shift or transformation. Of course, it is imaginable that, owing to a relatively low level of economic modernization, it is absolutely not easy for them to handle the relationship among the three types of aforementioned capitals.

The Case of Fuzhou City, Jiangxi Province

It is in the aforementioned discursive context that the exploratory practice of eco-civilization construction in Fuzhou city, Jiangxi Province, China, attracted our attention. On 26–29 April 2018, a research group mainly from Peking University and *Donghua* University of Technology, with the support of Rosa Luxemburg Foundation Beijing, conducted a field study on the theme of "Eco-capital, green technology and public participation in the socialist eco-civilization construction" at Fuzhou City, an eco-civilization pilot area of Jiangxi Province. Within three days, we carried out on-the-spot investigations to the following four examples. They are (1) "*Runbang* Agriculture" at Dongxiang District, a privately operated modern ecological production and management complex which was once a state-run farm; (2) "*Feitianfeng* Eco-breeding" at Linchuan District, a private enterprise of organic poultry farming which began its business with renting the wasteland in the village at a low price; (3) "The City Eco-cloud Data Information Platform" (as well as the related "*Lübao*" Carbon GSP Public Service Platform), a recently hot technical innovation of public management based on the idea of attracting more people to know more about the environmental situation around them;

(4) "The Fenggang River Wetland", a successful reconstruction project of urban water ecological landscape, which changed from a smelly foul water into an attractive landscape belt.

What is common among the four examples are the very high visibility and active interaction among eco-capital, green technology, and public participation or involvement in the process of eco-civilization construction, as my Chinese colleagues[22] have vividly described. On this basis, we may further raise the following three questions regarding how these examples are broadening and deepening our understandings of and/or expectations from the relationships of eco-capital, green technology, and public participation and of eco-capital, cultural capital, and industrial capital, from an eco-Marxist perspective, for instance.

(1) Leading role of the local governments and its implementation mechanisms: Imaginably, local governments at different levels will play the role of a comprehensive organizer or guarantor in encouraging the development (inventing) of eco-capital and cultural capital, attracting societal industry and commerce capital into the field of eco-capital and cultural capital development and supporting the development, management and accumulation of these "green capitals" with favorable policies and administrative measures, just like what they have done in actively encouraging and promoting the development of township enterprises 40 years ago at the beginning of reform and opening-up. But more noteworthily today, in what sense and through what ways should governments at different levels at the same time do well in the national (regional) policy and plan guidance in line with

[22] Huajie Cai, "Reflections of the Ecologicalization Mechanism of Capital," *Journal of Poyang Lake,* 5(2018): 58–62; Qihe Hua, "The Fuzhou Experience of Socialist Eco-Civilization Construction with Chinese Characteristics," *Theory and Review,* 4(2018): 52–56; Changhua Jü, "The Application of Technology and the Mechanism of Public Participation," *Theory and Review,* 4(2018): 49–51; Qiang Li, "Public Participation in the Process of Capital Ecologicalization: Taking Fuzhou City as an Example," *Journal of Poyang Lake,* 5(2018): 52–57.

vigorously promoting the eco-civilization construction, and as far as possible ensure or attract the institutionalized democratic participation of the people who are affected in this way or another? As for the policy and plan guidance, the most important thing is to integrate the national policies and strategies such as Eco-civilization Pilot Areas (*shengtai wenming shiyanqu*), Rural Revitalization (*xiangcun zhenxing*) and Beautiful Rural Construction (*meili xiangcun jianshe*), Construction of Small Towns (*xiaochengzhen jianshe*), Targeted Poverty Alleviation (*jingzhun fupin*), and so on, so as to achieve a comprehensive effect of policy. For the institutionalized democratic participation, the most important thing is to try to extend the business or economic participation or involvement in a narrow sense (through investment and employment) into a social, economic and political participation or involvement that is as wide as possible.

(2) Innovations of the systems and mechanisms to promote the eco-civilization construction and their extensibility and applicability: Undoubtedly, what is most to be expected from the aforementioned two interactive practices of "capitals" is whether and how they can bring about institutional and mechanism innovations of reconstruction in the process of vigorously promoting the eco-civilization construction in China. For the first time, the working report to the 19th National Congress of CPC clearly proposed that China will build an "Ecological environmental governance system with governments as the major player, enterprises as the subject of liabilities, social organizations and the public as the co-participants."[23] Therefore, a more scientific public management in environmental economy and environmental administration of the aforementioned two interactive relations will certainly turn out to be an important methodological approach and a great promoting power in creating a strong and effective ecological governance system. Moreover, the practical exploration at the local levels will definitely be very diversified and vivid. Of course,

[23] Jinping Xi, *The Working Report to the 19th Congress of CPC*. Beijing: People's Press, 2017a.

in theory at least, we also have to consider the other (or several) possibility. For instance, due to the lack of necessary or appropriate general social-economic conditions and regulation mechanisms, the actual capitalization of ecological and/or cultural elements and their thriving economic development eventually fail to become a green innovator or re-constructor of traditional industrial and commercial capital. Instead, it becomes just another form of the general capital (green capital), thus unable to play a preconceived role of promoting/safeguarding the ecological sustainability. Similarly, in terms of social sustainability, eco-capital or cultural capital is ultimately to be a driving force for further economic and social differentiation in local communities, rather than a practical path toward the beautiful future visions such as New Socialist Countryside (*shehuizhuyi xin nongcun*), *Beautiful Country* (meili xiangcun), New Type of Towns and Villages (*xinxing chengzhenhua*), and so on.

(3) Development of the model enterprises (communities) and their demonstration leading role: Enterprises and local communities are the constitutive "social cells" that practice and realize institutional or system innovations in the two interactive relations analyzed previously. Moreover, in the discursive context of eco-civilization construction, they become more closely related. That is because, on the one hand, the development and application of eco-capital, cultural capital, and green technology is inseparable from the understanding and support of the surrounding and related communities, for the development of economic activities as such almost inevitably relates to the various ecological (cultural and historical) resources and the urban and rural environmental quality (cultural life) of the surrounding or affected areas and communities. Arguably, compared to the traditional industrial production and operation, the so-called "Green economic activities" are more directly related to natural eco-systems (cultural heritages) of the surrounding or affected areas and communities. On the other hand, the degree of civilization and the comprehensive development level of local communities will also have direct impact on the development and

application of eco-capital, cultural capital, and green technology in the local areas, especially on their selection of direction and specific forms. It can be expected that the higher the overall quality and capacity of regulation and participation of local communities, the more likely the development and application of eco-capital, cultural capital, and green technology promote a higher level of ecological and social sustainability. Accordingly, the local society as a whole will more actively adopt the economic and technological forms with strong "green" or "red green" characteristics, and the enterprises will pay more attention to the government's environmental regulations, their own green enterprise image and the ecological and social responsibilities in the process of production and operation. For that matter, besides the rapid and healthy growth of the enterprises, all the institutional and policy innovations being conducive to a constructive interaction between enterprises and communities deserve our special attention.

Corresponding to the order of the three questions raised earlier, our major findings from the field-study in Fuzhou City, Jiangxi Province, can be briefly summarized as follows. Firstly, party committees and governments at different levels and their subordinate departments are indeed prioritizing the development of eco-capital, cultural capital, and green technology on their daily agenda, taking it as both a symbolic measure and a practical approach in implementing the CPC's up-to-date political ideology and the national strategy of vigorously promoting eco-civilization construction. A good example of this is that a Deputy Director of the Publicity Department of the CPC Municipal Committee is directly involved in the enterprise image promotion and product marketing of "*Feitianfeng* Eco-breeding" at Linchuan District, which is actually a private enterprise of organic poultry farming.

Secondly, both the development and application of "The City Eco-cloud Data Information Platform" as well as the related "*Lübao*" Carbon GSP Public Service Platform and the construction of "The Fenggang River Wetland" are achieving remarkable progress in attracting and safeguarding public participation or involvement in the eco-civilization construction. For instance, residents can get involved in the democratic supervision of local environmental quality and the following-up policymaking process through "earning green consumption points" in their daily lives, which is based on the idea that your environment-friendly behavior of consumption will bring you some free or cheaper commodities.[24] In just about half a year — from August 2017 to January 2018, the registered users of "*Lübao*" Carbon GSP Public Service Platform reached 162 000, 4% of the total population of Fuzhou.

Thirdly, the major efforts of improving the public service for and strengthening the economic administration of such emerging eco-agribusinesses like "*Runbang* Agriculture" and "*Feitianfeng* Eco-breeding" associated with various forms of big data information platforms are showing tremendous potential for institutional innovation, going far beyond what they were originally defined or understood as, such as the issues of administrative law enforcement information disclosure and "Three rural problems" (*san nong wenti*). Rather, they put forward or point out a series of issues profoundly reforming the urban and rural public governance systems as well as their capacity building, such as the coordinated enforcement of informatization, specialization, and democratization of urban ecological management, the new dynamics and new paths of rural economic development and the new forms of realization of natural value. It is reasonable to believe that, all the new understandings to and proper dealing with these issues will to a large extent reshape our current knowledge of eco-civilization construction and the concept of eco-civilization itself. In short, the rapid rise of eco-agricultural enterprises

---

[24] Of course, from an ecologist perspective, it is not good or strong enough to make the common people to do the ecologically right things by attracting or tempting them to do so with more or less economic benefits (Andrew Dobson, *Citizenship and the Environment*. Oxford: Oxford University Press, 2003). However, within a favorable societal environment and with necessary appropriate measures, these initial economic benefits-motivated behaviors might eventually become new living habits of the new generations.

(as the production and management complex) like "*Runbang* Agriculture" and "*Feitianfeng* Eco-breeding" provides us with an unprecedented richness of political imagination of the new pattern of agricultural economy and the new scene of rural life in the context of socialist eco-civilization construction, which can be to some extent regarded as an affirmation of my assumption about "Green development approach(strategy)" of the eco-civilization construction.[25]

Undoubtedly, there are lots of difficulties and challenges in front of the pioneering "Green enterprises" and the pilot areas of eco-civilization construction like Fuzhou City, Jiangxi Province.[26] Among them, to make these Green enterprises a mainstream enterprise and economic model, it will need a much longer time for their own efforts, together with some fundamental changes of the general social–economic system (such as the national economic performance evaluation system), while their seemingly immature even naïve operating environment (such as the relatively simple factory building and hardware facilities) and marketing strategies (such as the relatively weak consciousness of brand and its simplicity of publicity) today actually contain different directions of evolution in the future. Perhaps even more importantly, what pattern of relationship configuration with the surrounding communities (including residents) will "*Runbang* Agriculture" and "*Feitianfeng* Eco-breeding" — starting their business respectively from reconstructing an originally state-run farm and renting a wasteland in the village — evolve into eventually? Though, it is true that for the moment relationship between the two sides are relatively harmonious — "*Runbang* Agriculture" hires a large number of residents from the local communities as its full-time

[25] Qingzhi Huan, "The Green Development Path for Eco-Civilization Construction: A Case of Jiangxi Province," *Journal of Poyang Lake,* 1(2017b): 29–41.

[26] Huajie Cai, "Reflections of the Ecologicalization Mechanism of Capital," *Journal of Poyang Lake,* 5(2018): 58–62; Changhua Jü, "The Application of Technology and the Mechanism of Public Participation," *Theory and Review,* 4(2018): 49–51; Qiang Li, "Public Participation in the Process of Capital Ecologicalization: Taking Fuzhou City as an Example," *Journal of Poyang Lake,* 5(2018): 52–57.

or part-time workers, while "*Feitianfeng* Eco-breeding" takes up numerous villages adjacent to it into its product business chain.

Concluding Remarks

The major argument of this chapter is that, within an appropriate discursive and institutional system of socialist eco-civilization, introduction and application of eco-capital and green technology can turn out to be a promoting force of incorporating the local people into the emerging green industries or economy in China. Moreover, with such a society (rather than capital or capitalists)-oriented constructive interaction among them — eco-capital, green technology, and public participation — may enhance or reshape the process of dealing with the various forms of environmental problems into a long journey toward a green future of eco-civilization. Of course, the analysis of the case of Fuzhou City, Jiangxi Province, just one instance out of many in today's China, has clearly shown that there is no guarantee that this green development strategy or approach for eco-civilization construction is or will definitely be a success. Among the many affecting factors, the following two deserve our long-term observation and attention. Firstly, to what extent and in what ways can socialist political principles and institutional conditions be better persisted and implemented in these pioneering areas of eco-civilization construction. A key question to be answered is why are these economically backward areas — according to conventional standards — appropriate for practicing such socialist and/or ecologist ideals? Secondly, to what extent and in what ways are these pioneering areas for eco-civilization construction allowed to operate their eco-capital and green technology along different principles or logics of economic management? As the case of Fuzhou City has shown us, the first round of eco-capital and green technology are often not from the local communities, instead, they are from the developed areas like Shanghai, Beijing or Nanjing. Therefore, it would be very difficult for them to introduce and insist on a new principle of enhancing ecological sustainability rather than doing business as usual.

https://doi.org/10.1142/9789811225222_0005

Chapter 5

The Sustainable Energy Development Strategy in the LAO PDR

Ekto Vongphakdy

Institute of Foreign Affairs, Lao PDR

Introduction

Basically, the affordable energy services are among the essential ingredients of economic development for any country, including eradication of extreme poverty as called for in the United Nations Sustainable Development Goals (SDGs). Modern energy services mainly provided by liquid and gaseous fuels, as well as electricity, are essential for building enterprises and creating jobs. Convenient, affordable energy is also important for improving health and education, for reducing drudgery of conventional cooking, and for meeting other basic needs.

Meeting these essential energy needs economically and sustainably requires a balanced energy portfolio that is suited to the economic, social, and resource conditions of individual countries and regions. Renewable energy (RE) sources such as wind, solar, hydro, geothermal, and bio-energy thus have an important role to play, alongside fossil fuels, in an energy portfolio aimed at achieving sustainable development and inclusive growth of the nation.

Sustainable energy technologies face a number of barriers which cause delay in scaling up their production and use in the developing countries. Unlike conventional energy sources which have benefited from decades of research and development, established industrial base, and government subsidized infrastructure support, sustainable energy options are just gaining popularity in many regions. New policies can have a dramatic impact on the pace of introduction of RE, as several developing countries have demonstrated. This chapter presents a strategy for sustainable energy development, along with the challenges and opportunities for sustainable energy development in the current national enabling environment.

Country Profile

The Lao People's Democratic Republic (PDR) is a landlocked country of about 236,800 km^2, located in the heart of the Indochina Peninsula. The country is divided into 17 provinces and Vientiane is the capital. Its longest borders are those with Thailand to the west and Vietnam to the east; it is also bordered by China to the north, Cambodia to the south and Myanmar to the northwest.

The country stretches 1,700 km north to south and between 140 and 500 km from east to west. The Lao PDR is heavily forested and mountainous. There is an abundance of rivers, including a 1,900 km section of the Mekong River (Nam Khong). The terrain comprises mostly rugged mountains, with the highest point at 2,820 m, which gives the country good hydroelectric potential. Forest and woodland cover 47% of the land area.

The Lao PDR also has natural resources, including coal, hardwood timber, hydropower, gypsum, tin, gold, and gemstones. These resources all play a significant part in the economy. The country has a tropical monsoon climate, and experiences three distinct seasons. The cool season lasts from October to February, when the average temperature drops to about 16°C. The hot season is from the end of February to April when the temperature in the south can reach 40°C. The rest of the year is the rainy monsoon season. The mountainous

regions experience more than 10° cooler temperatures, and these regions can become very cold during winters. In January, highland temperatures can drop to even 0°C.

The Lao PDR is a country rich in natural resources, which is traditionally agrarian, but is now in a transition phase, becoming more urbanized, with a market-oriented economy increasingly integrated with neighboring countries in the Greater Mekong Sub-region. Between 2002 and 2019, the Lao PDR has experienced robust

Table 1 Key economic indicators as of 2019

Indicators	Values	Unit
Land area	236,800	Km^2
Population	7.16	Million
GDP	19.13	Billion KN
GDP per Capita	2,670	USD

Note: https://www.imf.org/external/datamapper/profile/LAO/WEO.

economic growth averaging 7–8% annually. Mining and hydropower investments have increased significantly in recent years, making important contributions to the economic growth (Table 1).

Energy Resources[1,2]

Conventional sources of energy

Coal and Lignite: The Lao PDR's coal reserves are estimated to be about 600–700 million tons, occurring mostly as lignite with smaller amounts of anthracite. The largest reserve of lignite has been found in Hongsa in Xayaboury Province; it is estimated to contain about 400 million tons, or more than half the estimated total reserves of the country. The mid-grade lignite is suitable for electricity generation and meets other industrial thermal energy requirements. Coal consumption is currently limited to cement factories, using about 35,000 tons per year, and a few other smaller users.

Oil and Gas: No excavation is available on oil and natural gas in the Lao PDR.

[1] National Assessment Framework on Enabling Environment, Technology Innovation Ecosystem for making Sustainable Energy options Affordable and Accessible — Report prepared by National Consultants, the Lao PDR.

[2] Asian Development Bank, Independent Evaluation Department, Sector Assistance Program Evaluation for the Energy Sector in the Lao PDR.

RE sources and applications

Hydropower: The Mekong river sub-basins in the Lao PDR have an estimated 20,000 MW of technically viable hydropower potential. By 2018, 2,971 MW of this capacity has been developed and has been operational for both domestic consumption and export. Another project under construction has a total installed capacity of 6,054 MW, in which independent power producer (IPP) export accounts for 4,413 MW; and domestic use for 1,495.5 MW.

Additionally, 75 new hydropower projects are in various stages of study, approval, and design. Hydropower plants (HPPs) provide electricity both to domestic customers (through the grid) and foreign markets (Thailand and Vietnam).

Small Hydropower: Hydropower installations in the Lao PDR with capacity less than 15 MW are considered as small hydro. The estimated potential for small hydropower in the Lao PDR is around 2,000 MW. To date, around 30 MW capacity projects have been developed, out of which 19.7 MW capacity projects are connected to the grid. Projects with a total capacity of 82.7 MW are currently under construction.

Biomass: Every year, the agriculture and forestry sectors produce large amounts of waste, such as rice straw and husks, sawdust, and corn cobs. The annual energy potential of this waste is estimated at 500 million tons of oil equivalent (mtoe), which can be used as feedstock for power generation. So far, biomass is only used at the household level, and more than 80% of the population still relies on biomass energy, especially for cooking. Biomass is also used for small-scale rural industrial production (e.g., alcohol production and tobacco processing). The country also has high potential for bio-fuel production from oily crops such as jatropha, oil palm, and soybean. The estimated potential from biogas and solid waste resources is around 313 MW and 216 MW, respectively. The Lao PDR is developing a national program on bio-fuel development, with a vision to introduce 10% bio-fuel in the transport sector by 2025.

Solar: The Lao PDR has an average of 200–300 sunlight days per year, with more sunlight days in the south. The potential capacity of solar energy is estimated at around 4.5–5 kilowatt-hours (kWh) per square meter (m^2) per day. Solar power has the potential to play a major role in providing off-grid electric power for remote rural areas. At present, around 13,000 households, mostly in remote areas have been supplied with solar home systems. However, limited progress has been made in the grid-connected solar sector, with only one existing rooftop solar photovoltaic (PV) system (of 236 kW capacities) installed at Wattay International Airport.

Wind Power: Scientific wind resource assessment for identifying the wind power potential has not yet been undertaken in the Lao PDR. The preliminary GIS base resource assessment study conducted by WISE reveals 4–5 m/s wind speed at 80 m hub height.

The Lao Government has signed a memorandum of understanding (MoU) with Impact Energy Asia Limited for conducting wind resource assessment in the Lao PDR. The basic feasibility studies conducted at two sites in Savannakhet Province indicate the wind power potential of 64 MW.

Primary and Final Energy Consumption

The primary energy source in the Lao PDR, as in many developing countries in the region, is biomass. In terms of final energy use, biomass accounts for less than 60%, petroleum products account for about 17%, electricity for 12%, and charcoal and coal for 14% (Figure 1).

Sector-wise Energy Consumption

In 2018, total final energy consumption was 2,336 kilotons of oil equivalent (ktoe). Households account for 51% of total final energy consumption, the transport sector for 26%, the industrial sector for 20%, agriculture sectors 2%, and commercial sector 1%. The high

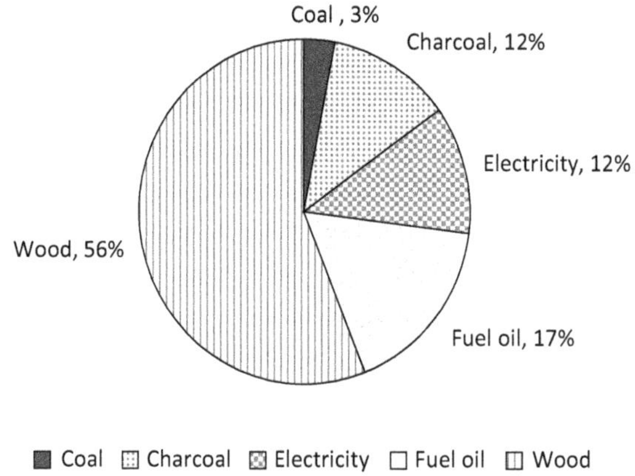

Figure 1 Final Energy Use by Source

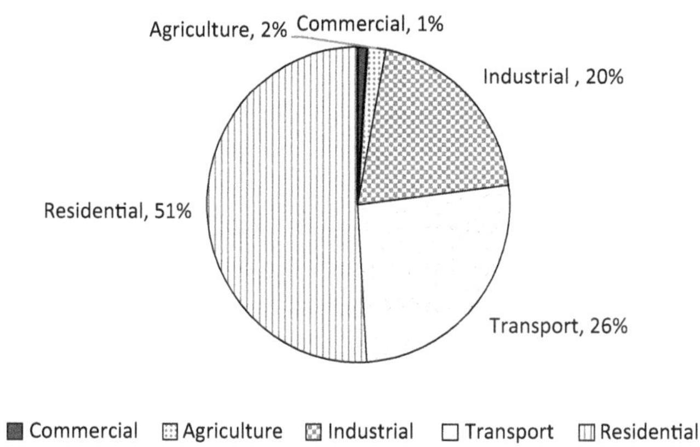

Figure 2 Sector-wise Energy Consumption

share accounted for by households reflects their reliance on biomass, which has low efficiency. The sector-wise consumption also reflects the relatively low level of industrial and commercial activity. While petroleum fuels are used for transport and industry, they are also used to generate electricity by households yet to be connected to the grid. All petroleum fuels are imported (Figure 2).

Table 2 Installed capacity of power generation projects

Source	Installed Capacity (MW)
Hydro	2978.17
Biomass	39.74
Diesel	1.491
Solar	0.873
Total	3020.27

Source: National report of the Ministry of Energy and Mines (MEM) 2018.

Installed Capacity of Power Projects in MW

The current installed capacity of power generation projects stands at 3020.27 MW as on February 2018. The energy mix is dominated by hydro (98.61%). The hydropower projects consist of projects installed by Electricité du Laos (EdL, an electrical utility in Lao), those set up by IPPs for domestic use, and for export purpose (Table 2).

Access to Grid Electricity

As on December 2013, a total of 943,599 households out of 1,080,342 were electrified across the country, which means that 87.34% households were electrified. Out of this, about 2% were electrified by RE-based/hybrid off-grid systems. This indicates that there are 1,696 villages in which 136,743 households (12.66%) remain un-electrified, located in the remote, less dense parts of the country.

Energy Demand[3]

Future energy demand has been projected to increase at an annual average rate of 6.7% for real GDP growing at an annual average of rate of 7.1% for the period 2010–2025; therefore, GDP elasticity to energy is 0.94. Coal and electricity will expand their shares from 4.4%

[3] National Assessment Framework on Enabling Environment, Technology Innovation Ecosystem for making Sustainable Energy options Affordable and Accessible — Report prepared by National Consultants, the Lao PDR.

Table 3 Energy demand by source (in ktoe)

Source	2000	2010	2015	2020	2025
Coal	0	106	355	746	1,268
Petroleum products	272	592	981	1,355	1,781
Biodiesel	0	0	0	46	127
Bioethanol	0	0	0	11	27
Electricity	55	210	393	633	927
Fuel wood	1,103	1,386	1,561	1,752	1,954
Charcoal	71	128	174	226	279
Total	**1,502**	**2,442**	**3,464**	**4,769**	**6,364**

Source: National report of the MEM 2018.

Table 4 Energy demand by sector (in ktoe)

Sector	2000	2010	2015	2020	2025
Industry	63	232	615	1,193	1,977
Transportation	266	564	939	1,354	1,859
Commercial	210	332	431	528	611
Residential	959	1,269	1,466	1,651	1,865
Agriculture	3	21	26	30	35
Non-energy	0	3	7	12	17
Total	**1,502**	**2,442**	**3,464**	**4,769**	**6364**

Source: National report of the MEM 2018.

in 2010 to 19.9% in 2025, and 8.7% in 2010 to 14.6% in 2025, respectively; however, these shares will still be only half of that of fuel wood and charcoal (35.1%) and petroleum products (28.0%).

By sector, the industrial sector, which is assumed to have high real GDP growth, will rapidly increase demand (annual average 15.3%), expanding its share from 9.6% (2010) to 31.1% (2025), which will be higher than the transportation sector (29.2% in 2025) and household (residential) sector (29.3% in 2025). On the other hand, the annual average increase in the rate of residential use will remain at 2.6% from 2010 to 2025. The energy demand by source and sector are illustrated in Tables 3 and 4.

Table 5 Demand forecast (in MW)

Year/ Consumers	2010	2011	2012	2013	2014	2015	2016	2017	2018	2019	2020
Residential	492	522	557	592	631	673	718	769	838	916	1,004
Factory	17	45	133	214	260	475	578	778	785	793	794
Mining	75	77	168	176	192	320	536	539	521	524	527
SEZ	—	—	10	35	58	70	116	120	180	180	210
Construction	—	24	33	27	159	395	311	143	147	70	41
Railway	—	92	120	120	120	49	21	21	21	21	21
Subtotal	584	758	1,021	1,165	1,420	1,982	2,281	2,371	2,492	2,504	2,597
SLACO	—	—	—	—	100	900	900	900	900	900	900
Total	**584**	**758**	**1,021**	**1,165**	**1,520**	**2,882**	**3,181**	**3,271**	**3,392**	**3,404**	**3,497**

Electricity Demand[4]

The demand for the residential sector is expected to grow gradually from year 2010 to 2020, with an average rate of about 7%. Non-residential demand is expected to increase substantially due to the rapid growth of demand from factories and mines. The average growth rate of non-residential demand, except SLACO, is 33% from 2010 to 2020 (Table 5).

Organization of the Energy Sector

Management of energy-related activities in the Lao PDR is looked after by the MEM, EdL, and Lao Holding State Enterprise (LHSE), with support from the Ministry of Finance and the Ministry of Natural Resources and the Environment (MONRE). The MEM is responsible for energy policy and overall strategic guidance, as well as management of sector development. The various departments under MEM are shown in Figure 3.

[4] National Assessment Framework on Enabling Environment, Technology Innovation Ecosystem for making Sustainable Energy options Affordable and Accessible — Report prepared by National Consultants, The Lao PDR.

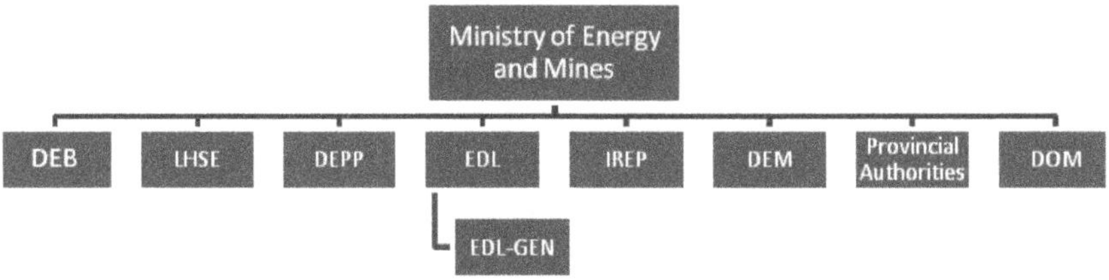

Figure 3 Organization Chart of MEM

Note: DEB: Department of Energy Business, LHSE: Lao Holding State Enterprise, DEPP: Department of Energy Policy and Planning, EDL: Electricité du Laos, EDL-GEN: EDL Generation Public Company, IREP: Institute of Renewable Energy Promotion, DEM: Department of Energy Management, DOM: Department of Mining.

The Electricity Law of the Lao PDR amended in year 2011 prescribes that the MEM is responsible for making the policy and strategy for the nation's electricity sector. The also has the responsibility to develop and implement laws and regulations, and to supervise the businesses of electricity companies. The task and responsibilities assigned to the various departments under the MEM are elaborated as follows.

Department of Energy Business (*DEB*): Formerly known as the Department of Energy Promotion and Development, the DEB is in charge of private sector investments in the power sector. DEB is responsible for overseeing the investment in transmission projects and coal-fired thermal power projects. While DEB is involved in planning, development, and appraisal of project proposals, its main role is negotiating project development agreements, concession agreements, and power purchase agreements. DEB's duties also include monitoring project implementation.

The department has four divisions: Administrative Division, Contract Division, Project Development Division, and Project Monitoring Division.

Department of Energy Policy and Planning (*DEPP*): DEPP is in charge of policymaking and planning, and is responsible for energy policymaking and energy/electricity supply planning.

Department of Energy Management (*DEM*): This newly created department is in charge of drafting energy-related laws, regulations, guidelines, and technical and safety standards. The DEM also monitors government agencies, state-owned enterprises, and private operators to ensure that they operate in accordance with the rules and regulations. Further, the DEM monitors the energy use of enterprises, factories, and buildings and presents energy awards to the most efficient users. Another important function of the DEM is inspecting the technical standards of electrical equipment and appliances, either domestically produced or imported. The department issues energy business licenses and approves or rejects extensions. The DEM also provides technical consultation services, and information on energy administration and management.

Institute of Renewable Energy Promotion (*IREP*): Equivalent to a department, the IREP is mainly responsible for promoting RE and conservation by implementing the Renewable Energy Policy and Strategy prepared in 2011. In support of RE, the IREP is tasked with developing small-scale hydro, biodiesel, and biogas projects, and with preparing a manual on RE production and use. In support of rural electrification, the institute formulates and implements a rural electrification master plan. In support of Energy Efficiency and Conservation (EEC), the IREP formulates regulations, guidelines, and a user's manual on EEC. Its conservation targets include developing more efficient cooking stoves and implementing a mechanism project on EEC.

Electricité du Laos (*EdL*): EdL is a state-owned electric power utility, supplying electricity to domestic consumers through its transmission and distribution lines. EdL also manages import and export of electricity. EdL owns transmission lines and distribution lines for domestic supply countrywide, obtains electricity from EdL-owned power stations, and imports from neighboring countries. EdL was initially a vertically integrated utility, which owned generation, transmission, and distribution facilities, and was responsible for generating, transmitting, and selling electricity. In 2010, following directives from the Government of Lao on restructuring the electricity industry in the country, the function of electricity generation was handed over to EdL-Gen Company.

EdL-Gen: EdL-Generation Public Company (*EdL-Gen*) was established on 15 December 2010 as the first publicly held enterprise in the Lao PDR listed on the Lao Securities Exchange (*LSX*). The main objectives of EdL-Gen are (1) to generate energy for EdL for wholesale, and in the future to export (this includes development of transmission lines and substations, as necessary), (2) to invest in or set up joint ventures with other electricity generation projects, and (3) to provide management and maintenance services for other electricity projects.

Lao Holding State Enterprise (*LHSE*): LHSE is a state-owned stock-holding enterprise established in 2005. The mission of LHSE is to hold and manage shares of IPP projects.

Besides the aforementioned departments/companies, the government of Lao has also set up the Provincial Department of Energy and Mines (PDEM) and District Energy and Mines Office (DEMO) which work under the MEM, at the provincial and district levels, respectively.

Energy Policy, Law, and Regulations

The Lao PDR does not have a comprehensive national energy policy setting out a systematic approach to energy planning, policy formulation, and sector development. However, the government has notified a Law on Electricity, as well as few policies/strategies for the development of large hydro and RE sources. Besides the Lao Electric Power Technical Standards and the grid code, the country does not have any regulation to manage the power sector operations.

Law on Electricity: The Law on Electricity for Lao was amended in 2011 and enacted on 20 December 2011 by replacing the earlier Law on Electricity notified on 8 December 2008. The Law on Electricity specifies the principles, rules, and measures on the organization, operation, management, and inspection of electrical activities for the high effectiveness of electricity generation and business operation with the aim to use the natural resource potential in an economical and sustainable manner, to encourage the implementation of the National Socio-Economic Development Plan (NSEDP), and to improve the living conditions of the multi-ethnic people. The Law is divided into 10 Chapters and 81 Articles specifying the principles and guidelines for conducting electricity generation, transmission, and distribution business in the Lao PDR. The Law also recommends the strategies for development of rural electrification network and methodologies for the pricing of electricity.

The 8th National Socio-Economic Development Plan (NSEDP) 2016–2020: The main objectives of the government's NSEDP include rapid economic growth and poverty eradication; achievement of the SDGs by 2030; graduation from least-developed country status by 2024; and sustainable economic, social, and environmental development. The 8th NSEDP identifies the energy sector as a strategic development sector, both for the short and longer terms. Its performance is vital for meeting the country's energy requirements, notably with respect to the still-elusive goal of nationwide electrification. Development of the sector is central to modernization and industrialization of the country, which is the primary basis for raising the living standards and poverty reduction.

Renewable Energy Development Strategy: The government of the Lao PDR launched the Renewable Energy Development Strategy in October 2011, which so far is the main policy framework for the development of RE in the country. The strategy targets to increase the share of RE in total energy consumption to 30% by 2025. The government also aims to replace 10% of transport fuels by bio-fuels during the same period, and the target details of each RE are illustrated in Table 6.

Policy on Sustainable Hydropower Development in the Lao PDR: The policy on sustainable hydropower development in the Lao PDR (PSHD) applies to all hydropower projects larger than 15 MW throughout the project development process (planning, construction, operation, and transfer/closure stages) and incorporates technical,

Table 6 RE capacity addition proposed in RE strategy

Item	Phase Description	2015 MW	2020 MW	2025 MW
1	Electricity	140	243	725
1.1	Small Hydropower	80	134	400
1.2	Solar	22	36	48
1.3	Biomass	13	24	58
1.4	Biogas	10	19	51
1.5	Municipal solid waste	9	17	36
1.6	Wind	6	12	73
2	Bio-fuels production	ML	ML	ML
2.1	Ethanol	15.42	34.62	97.6
2.2	Biodiesel	22.25	63.93	194.5
3	Heat	Ktoe	Ktoe	Ktoe
3.1	Biomass	23	29	113
3.2	Biogas	22	44	178
3.3	Solar	17	22	109

Source: National report of the MEM 2018.

engineering, economic and finance, environment and social impacts aspects. The PSHD is being reviewed by the MEM at present.

Power Development Plan (*PDP*): Article 9 of the Electricity Law states that the electricity enterprises shall prepare the electricity development plan. EdL has been preparing the PDP every 3–5 years. EdL formulated the PDP 2010–2020 in August 2010, revising the former PDP 2007–2017. In August 2011, EdL updated PDP 2010–2020 by reflecting the latest electricity demand forecast and prospective project developments in the generation and transmission sector.

Development of Regulation/law on Bio-fuels: The Lao PDR is developing a national program for bio-fuel development with a vision to introduce 10% bio-fuel in the transport sector by year 2025. Further, the (draft) Decree for regulation and utilization of bio-fuel in the Lao PDR, dated 11 September 2013 had classified the size of bio-fuel production and level of approval into three levels. Family business size production (less than 200 L per day) requires licensing approval by the Energy and Mine District Office in accordance with the agreed organizations concerned. Small to medium size of business production (capacity between 201 and 9,999 L per day) shall require licensing approval from the Energy and Mine Provincial Division, whereas large scale businesses with product capacity over 10,000 L per day shall require licensing approval by the MEM.

Electricity Market and Pricing Mechanism

EdL is a state-owned corporation under the MEM which owns and operates the country's main generation, transmission, and distribution assets in the Lao PDR, and manages electricity imports into its grids and exports from its stations. EdL also has a role in project development and has been the implementing agency for government hydropower power projects, and is also the government's shareholder in the case of IPP projects. It has been the past practice for EdL to take over from MEM the responsibility for a project, once a shareholder's agreement is executed and the project loans are closed.

EdL's own generating capacity is almost 100% hydro based. The utility has 10 hydropower projects totaling 390.7 MW capacities, mostly of small capacity (less than 50 MW). Its largest power plant is Nam Ngum 1 (155 MW), commissioned in 1971. EdL's own generation is insufficient for supplying to the domestic market; hence, it buys power from a number of domestic IPPs. Currently, the largest domestic IPP is the Nam Lik 1/2 HPP, with a capacity of 100 MW. The total capacity of IPPs supplying electricity to domestic use stands at 285 MW (Table 7).

Prior to 2019, EdL's operations in the Lao PDR's 17 provinces were divided into four areas — northern, central 1, central 2, and southern. Each area had a 115 kilovolt (kV) grid but they were not interconnected. During 2011–2019, the 115 kV network has been expanded and interconnected, consolidating to three areas (central 1 and 2 have been combined). In addition to EdL's network, the provincial authorities operate 85 mini grids, supplied either with diesel generators or small hydropower stations. These facilities primarily serve remote areas not yet connected to the EdL grid.

Table 7 Installed hydropower project capacity in the Lao PDR

HPP Owned by EDL		HPP Set up by IPPs for Domestic Use		HPP Set up by IPPs for Export	
Name of Project	Capacity (MW)	Name of Project	Capacity (MW)	Name of Project	Capacity (MW)
Nam Ngum-1 (155 MW)	155	Nam Lik 1/2	100	Theun Hinboun	220
Xe Labam (5 MW)	5	Nam Tha-3	1.2	Theun Hinboun Ext.	220
Nam Dong (1MW)	1	Nam Ngone	3.2	Houay Ho	152
Nam Xeset-1	45	Nam Phao	1.7	Nam Theun-2	1088
Nam Ko	1.5	Nam Ngum-5	120	Nam Ngum-2	615
Nam Leuk	60	Nam Gnouang	60	—	—
Nam Ngai	1.2	Tat Salen	3	—	—
Nam Mang-3	40	—	—	—	—
Xeset-2 (76 MW)	76	—	—	—	—
Nam Song Ext	6	—	—	—	—
Total	**390.7**	—	**285.3**	—	**2295**

Source: National report of the MEM 2018.

Electricity pricing mechanism

Electricity tariffs in the Lao PDR are framed by the government; there is no independent regulatory authority for tariff determination purpose. With regard to retail tariff, EdL submits a draft electricity tariff proposal to MEM, and the government of the Lao PDR approves modification of the tariff in principle. The cost plus methodology in deciding feed-in-tariff (FIT) is not practiced in determination of generation tariff for the RE sources of energy. At present, the tariff for sale of electricity from RE power projects is agreed based on the negotiations between power producers and power utility EdL.

The retail tariff determination of electricity is guided by the socio-economic conditions of the consumers, the types of use and of the user. The MEM consults other departments to study the electricity price structure of each type to be submitted to the government for consideration within each period. The electricity tariff is set in nine categories for low voltage supply, and four categories for medium voltage supply. The tariff for residential use and irrigation are set at a lower level than that for other categories of consumers. The residential tariff and agricultural tariff are cross-subsidized to some extent by the industrial and commercial consumers.

Fiscal and Financial Regime for Development of Energy Business[5,6]

As per the provision under the Investment Promotion Law of the Lao PDR, the government provides both financial and non-financial incentives to investors based on different promoted sectors and promoted zones.

- Tax holidays offered up to 10 years.
- Exemption from export duty on export products.
- Exemption from land lease or concession fee up to 15 years.
- Exemption from import duties and taxes on raw materials and capital equipment using for production.
- Additional tax holidays are available upon negotiation for large concession projects.

Foreign investments subject to the Foreign Investment Law pay an annual profit tax at a rate of 10%, 15%, and 20% according to the promotion zone (other investments are taxed at 35%). The Lao Government specifies three promotion zones based on geographical location and socio-economic conditions. The zones are as follows:

- Zone 1: Mountainous, plain, and plateau zones, with no economic infrastructure to facilitate investments.

[5] Investment Promotion Law 2009.
[6] Investment in the Lao PDR, KPMG Lao Company Limited, March 2009.

- Zone 2: Mountainous, plain, and plateau zones with a certain level of economic infrastructure suitable to accommodate investments to some extent.
- Zone 3: Mountainous, plain, and plateau zones with good infrastructure to support investments.

As far as investment in renewable and sustainable energy projects is concerned, there are no specific promotional incentives being offered by the government. However, for the sugar factories and biodiesel developers, the following incentives are allowed.

- Free import duty for production machinery, equipment, and raw materials;
- Free import duty for chemical materials necessary for bio-fuels production within seven years.

The Renewable Development Strategy of the Lao PDR mentioned that all investments in RE projects in the Lao PDR, including that for bio-fuels production, grid-connected or isolated systems, off-grid projects, and individual systems, are entitled to investment incentives under the Investment Law of the Lao PDR updated in 2019. The financial incentives include the following:

- Import duty free on production machinery, equipment, and raw materials;
- Import duty free on chemical materials necessary for bio-fuels production within 7 years.

Overview of the banking sector

The current financial sector in the country consists of four state-owned commercial banks, 12 private banks (8 international, 4 domestic), two joint venture banks, 3 affiliated banks, three insurance companies (of which two are representative offices), one National Treasury under the Ministry of Finance, and the Agriculture Promotion Bank (a government institution which grants loans for agricultural development).

Table 8 Snapshot of the banking sector in the Lao PDR

Banks	No.	Assets Millions USD	Deposits Millions USD	Loans Millions USD	Loan to Deposit Ratio (%)
State-owned Banks	4	1,486.98	1,035.95	654.29	63.16
Joint Venture Banks	2	138.65	77.20	80.73	104.58
Private Banks	4	152.58	134.78	97.77	72.54
Affiliated Banks	3	142.41	55.72	53.29	95.64
International Banks	8	284.96	117.32	152.86	130.29
Total	**21**	**2,205.59**	**1,420.97**	**1,038.95**	**73.11**

Note: National Assessment Framework on Enabling Environment, Technology Innovation Ecosystem for making Sustainable Energy options Affordable and Accessible — Report prepared by National Consultants, the Lao PDR.

Source: Bank of the Lao PDR 4th Quarter Review, 2017.

The state-owned banks dominate the banking sector, accounting for 67.41% of all banking sector assets, and 62.98% of all bank loans (as of the fourth quarter 2018). There are four state-owned commercial banks in the Lao PDR: Banque pour le Commerce Exterieur Lao (BCEL), Nayoby Bank, Agricultural Promotion Bank (APB), and Lao Development Bank (LDB).

Although banks have not adopted any specific policies for providing financial support to the sustainable energy/RE business, they have provided loan for the renewable energy projects. For example, the APB has supported several biogas and bio-fuel projects. The LDP is providing finance to the hydropower projects like "Namlong HPP" (Table 8).

Energy Conservation Initiative

Energy conservation (EC) in the Lao PDR is at an early stage. The government has yet to develop a comprehensive national strategy for EEC. There has been some assistance provided by multilateral and bilateral donors, most notably the World Bank's assistance to Rural Electrification Project concerning demand-side management.

With the creation of the Institute of Renewable Energy and Promotion (IREP), and the DEM under the MEM, EC initiatives are now expected to be more coordinated. The IREP is preparing a national EEC strategy and draft regulations, and the DEM is preparing requirements concerning monitoring of energy use and labeling for electricity appliances.

The EdL is promoting efficient use of electricity in government offices, residential, and industrial sectors by providing energy-efficient lamps and air conditioning systems, and improving awareness on energy efficiency by providing training, and through mass media.

Institutional and Human Resource Development Framework

The energy sector business including sustainable energy development work in the Lao PDR comes under the purview of the MEM. Implementation of RE/sustainable energy programs is looked after by the IREP. The Lao Women's Union, National University of Laos, and EdL are some other organizations which are involved in implementing RE and sustainable energy programs. In general, RE sources will most likely be developed under the direction of MEM (Table 9).

Key Findings: Challenges and Opportunities for Sustainable Energy Development in the Current National Enabling Environment

(1) The Lao PDR is immensely blessed with economically viable hydropower potential, one of the cleanest and least cost option for energy generation. The solar insolation level and traditional agrarian base of the country indicate ample solar and biomass resource availability. However, there is a gap with respect to scientific resource assessment studies for estimating the RE potential which has not been yet conducted in the country.

(2) The present planning approach of the government is largely focused on the development of hydropower potential in the

Table 9 Institutional and HR framework for sustainable energy development in the Lao PDR

No.	Name of the Institution	Function
1	Institute of Renewable Energy Promotion/ MEM	Implementation of RE Program in the Lao PDR in consultation with government. Promote and develop RE. Promote and develop rural electrification. Promote EEC. Develop and manage RE database and information.
2	Renewable Energy and New Materials Institute (REMI)/MOST	REMI plays the role of secretary to MOST in research, development, transfer, promotion, application, and service on Science and Technology. REMI plays a vital role in conducting research and development in an applied and adaptive research platform on RE technology in conjunction with traditional technology for demonstrative and dissemination applications of RE technology to support government guidelines, policies, and development programs. It is also involved in studying, researching, and selecting international progressive technologies suitable for the country in order to achieve national socio- economic development. It is also involved in transferring the successful result of research, adjustment or development on the science and technology within the country. MOST created REMI as a training center, and demonstration and research center promoting the development and use of renewable energy technologies (RETs). This institute will also offer training in the utilization of the various technologies to national technicians in the region.
3	PDEM	Provides provincial level support for the implementation of RE and EEC.
4	Faculty of Engineering, National University of Laos	It is mainly involved with research and educational issues on RE; over 200 students have graduated in this field since 2000s.

Table 9 (*Continued*)

No.	Name of the Institution	Function
5	Faculty of Science, National University of Laos	Mainly involved with research and education issues on RE.
6	Lao Institute for Renewable Energy (LIRE)	Consultancy, conducting research, and providing RE technological (pico hydro, biodiesel, biogas, improved cookedstoves, rural energy), socio-economic, and energy efficiency services. Providing public resources for information and advice on the use of RE technologies. Capacity building and training related to RE.
7	Ministry of Natural Resources and Environment (MONRE)	Main coordinating agency for environmental planning and management across all sectors.
8	Renewable Energy for Sustainable Development Association of Lao (RESDALAO), Sunlabob	Private sector organizations, heavily involved in the introduction of RE equipment using innovative mechanisms such as hire purchase scheme for PV systems, solar powered water pumping, etc.

country. The government encourages hydropower development through IPPs for export purpose.

(3) Power export to neighboring countries is an important policy objective of the Lao government. Revenues generated from power export in the form of royalties, taxes, and dividends are important income sources for Lao.

(4) There are gaps in creating a comprehensive national energy policy defining the national goal, implementation plan, and strategies for sectoral development.

(5) The MEM is the main authority responsible for the management of energy sector, including the development of RE in the Lao PDR. The IREP under MEM oversees the implementation of RE, energy efficiency, and rural electrification programs in the Lao PDR.

(6) EdL is a vertically integrated state sector utility responsible for generation, transmission, and distribution of electricity in Laos. As of 2013, around 85% of the households in Lao have access to grid electricity; the remaining 15% households are located in relatively remote and inaccessible areas where extension of grid may not be economically viable.

(7) The government announced the "Renewable Energy Development Strategy" (REDS) for the Lao PDR during October 2011. The REDS aims to increase the share of RE to 30% of the total energy consumption by year 2025 in final energy terms. However, a gap exists in the system as there is no clear RE policy and implementation plan to back REDS.

(8) REDS is more focused on the promotion and development of bio-fuels to be used as transportation fuel. However, there are gaps in REDS as it does not suggest any clear strategy for promotion of other off-grid sustainable energy options/services.

(9) In terms of final energy consumption, share of biomass resource is around 60% indicating wider use of biomass for meeting the cooking and heating energy requirements. Future energy demand projection shows an increase in transportation and industrial demand. This makes a case for RE-based solutions in residential, industrial, and transportation sectors.

(10) No independent "Electricity Regulator" fills gaps in the system for tariff determination and monitoring the power sector operations in Lao. The tariff for sale of electricity from RE generating stations to the utility EdL is decided by the latter through negotiations with the RE generator on case-to-case basis. The retail tariff structure is finalized by the MEM. The residential and agricultural tariff is cross-subsidized by the industrial and commercial sector tariff. For many years, however, the electricity tariff has been set at a low level, undermining EdL's financial position.

(11) The Law on Electricity for Lao 2011 specifies the principles, rules, and procedures for managing power sector activities in the Lao PDR. The law on electricity has gaps as it does not have any enabling provisions for promotion of sustainable energy options in Lao; however, the Law mentions the need for encouraging

renewable sources of energy, as well as the use of off-grid RE sources for rural electrification.

(12) No special financial/fiscal incentives for encouraging sustainable energy options are available which creates gaps in investment environment. As per Investment Promotion Law of the Lao PDR, the investors including the sustainable energy investor are eligible for obtaining some fiscal/non-financial incentives like tax holidays, exemption of fee on concession agreement, etc.

(13) There are gaps in the Banking sector in Lao as it is not sensitized enough about the need for promoting sustainable energy sources and incentivizing such projects by offering soft loan, and longer repayment periods.

(14) The Lao government has successfully implemented few off-grid RE-based rural electrification programs with the help of international funding (World Bank, JICA) wherein, the use of solar home lighting systems has been successfully demonstrated in rural un-electrified areas. The public–private partnership mechanisms like those of Provincial Energy Service Companies (PESCO) and Sunlabob (Laos based full-service energy-provider selling hardware and providing commercially viable energy services for remote areas) have been successfully implemented.

(15) The government so far has not integrated RE into the national agenda such as the Socio-Economic Development Plan, Rural Electrification Plan, industrialization and modernization strategy, etc., which creates gap in the system for promoting sustainable energy technology.

(16) EC in the Lao PDR is at an early stage. The government is yet to develop a comprehensive national strategy for EEC.

(17) There are gaps in financing RE as budgetary provision from own resources is limited. The government so far relies mostly on the international funding and donor contribution to support RE programs in country.

(18) There is presence of government academic institutions, international institutes working on RE, private entrepreneurs providing energy services in rural areas; however, proper coordination and sharing of knowledge seem to be missing.

In conclusion, the Lao PDR's overall energy development strategy along with policies, incentives, electricity market structure have been discussed elaborately to highlight the opportunities that exist in the enabling environment. However, there are certain gaps that create hindrances in promotion of sustainable energy in the country. Meanwhile analysis of enabling environment is necessary, and its effectiveness in promoting sustainable energy technologies should also be addressed.

https://doi.org/10.1142/9789811225222_0006

Chapter

6

Lao Perspective: "Environmental Protection in ASEAN and China: Challenges and Cooperation"

Sulathin Thiladej

The Institute of Foreign Affairs (IFA), Laos

Introduction

Laos is one of the fastest growing economies in the dynamic Southeast Asian region. This growth is largely driven by the utilization of the country's abundant natural resources, including land, mineral, and water resources. However, such growth is found to be unsustainable, having impacts on the environment, which are changing rapidly and adversely. The most critical concerns over environmental sustainability are intertwined with degradation of forests, pollution of soil and water, and lack of individual awareness and community waste management. This chapter examines the pressing issues of environmental degradation in Laos and the major challenges associated with experiences in policymaking and implementation, and also provides policy implications on ASEAN member countries and China.

Southeast Asia is a diverse region, where almost all countries are rich in natural resources, and have been exploited to boost economic growth. Laos, which is land-locked and categorized as a least-developed country (LDC), has made use of its abundant natural resources for development, although there have been arguments on whether the natural resources' contribution to development is positive or negative.[1] Regardless of such arguments, Laos has made remarkable progress in development over the years, which is shown by the steady average GDP growth rate of 6–7% annually. The GDP per capita has risen remarkably over the past few decades with the recent GDP per capita reaching $2,577.[2] This progress in development is expected to enable Laos to achieve its targets for graduating from LDC status by 2024 and becoming a high middle-income country by 2030.[3] It is discovered that natural resources significantly contribute to such economic achievements through export-driven policy in the fields of agriculture, forestry, mineral, construction, and hydropower sectors.[4]

---

[1] E. Paltseva and J. Roine, "Are Natural Resources Good or Bad for Development," Policy Brief, Free Network, 2011, accessed October 12, 2019. https://freepolicybriefs.org/2011/11/21/are-natural-resources-good-or-bad-for-development/.

[2] World Bank, "Overview," The World Bank in Lao PDR, 2019, accessed April 29, 2019. https://www.worldbank.org/en/country/lao/overview.

[3] NIER (National Institute for Economic Research), "The Regional and International Integration and Connectivity Vision of the Lao PDR," in the EEC Development and Transport Facilitation Measures in Thailand, and the Development Strategies by the Neighboring Countries, BRC Research Report. JETRO Bangkok/IDE-JETRO: Bangkok Research Center, 2019.

[4] UN (United Nations), "Country Analysis Report: Lao PDR," Analysis to Inform the Lao People's Democratic Republic — United Nations Partnership Framework (2017–2021), United Nations in Vientiane, Lao PDR, 2015, accessed 30 April 2019. https://www.undp.org/content/dam/laopdr/docs/Reports%20and%20publications/2015/Country%20Analysis%20Report%20Lao%20PDR%202015.pdf; World Bank, "Lao PDR's Green Growth Reforms get $40 Million Boost with Credit from World Bank," The World Bank IBRD-IDA, 2019b, accessed 19 October 2019. https://www.worldbank.org/en/news/press-release/2019/05/28/lao-pdrs-green-growth-reforms-get-40-million-boost-with-credit-from-world-bank.

The pursuit of the national development plans, emphasizing foreign direct investment as one of the priorities, has recently brought in a wide range of projects through overseas investors to improve infrastructure connectivity nationwide such as the construction or upgradation of roads and bridges and electricity supply. This contributes to bettering livelihoods of people, especially those residing in rural areas by having better access to basic facilities including public health care services, education, and other opportunities for their well-being and improvement.[5] Laos, one of the world's least developed countries, is paying special attention to addressing national poverty. The recent poverty rate was about 23%, which is the second-highest poverty rate in Southeast Asia, after that is Myanmar, which is 32%.[6] However, such developments have not been achieved in a sustainable manner, resulting in myriad environmental issues such as deforestation, the deteriorated quality of soil and water resources, limited individual environmental awareness, and ineffective management of community wastes.

Like several other countries in the region, the most critical concern in Laos is deforestation, because forests have been decimated nationwide with weak public management in the exploitation of forest resources for boosting economic growth. Laos has 236,800 square kilometers of total land area, in which the uplands accounts for two-thirds and about 10% of total land area has been exploited for agricultural activities.[7] The national forest coverage accounts for around 40% in 2015 and this has significantly declined from the period of 1980s,

---

[5] MAF (Ministry of Agriculture and Forestry), Environmental and Social Management Framework. Vientiane, Lao PDR: Lao PDR Agriculture Commercialization Project (LACP), Ministry of Agriculture and Forestry, 2017.

[6] S. Khidhir, "Empty Bellies in Lao," The ASEAN Post, 2019, accessed September 13, 2019. https://theaseanpost.com/article/empty-bellies-lao.

[7] MONRE (Ministry of Natural Resources and Environment), "Lao Environment Outlook 2012," Ministry of Natural Resources and Environment, Vientiane, Lao PDR, 2012, accessed April 26, 2019. https://data.opendevelopmentmekong.net/dataset/be0addb0-adfa-484c-88c2-32a9219db511/resource/9c1229cb-25e4-4cbb-be23-2121c0012a50/download/lao_eo_2012.pdf.

which was above 50% of the total forest area.[8] A number of data show a decline in forest coverage and the quality and ecosystem function has been gradually deteriorating over the past few decades, for instance, the loss of forest cover was recorded as 12,759 hectares in 2015 compared to the loss of 6,478 hectares in 2010 and 2,314 hectares in 2006, respectively.[9] According to Food and Agricultural Organization (FAO),[10] the primary forest in Laos remains roughly 6% whereas the rest of the forest's percentage is under natural regeneration after being degraded. The forest cover decline is attributed to a wide range of factors; however, the key drivers are illegal logging practice, infrastructure projects including construction of roads and reservoirs, and the conversion of forest lands for agriculture and rural development projects.[11] Forest resource is an integral part of national socio-economic development and livelihoods of those dwelling in rural areas. Data demonstrates that the forestry rents contributed 3.8% to GDP in 2016.[12] Forests also provide invaluable non-timber

---

[8] ODL (Open Development Laos), "Environmental and Natural Resources," An East–West Management Institute Project, Open Development Initiative, 2019, accessed April 20, 2019. https://laos.opendevelopmentmekong.net/topics/environment-and-natural-resources/.

[9] *Ibid.*

[10] FAO, "Global Forest Resources Assessment 2015," Food and Agriculture Organization of the United Nations, Rome, 2015, accessed April 28, 2019. https://data.opendevelopmentmekong.net/dataset/0557389a-2e89-4a31-83f7-1a354eeec40b/resource/4077104b-0d7e-4f78-b3d1-d749e2310822/download/a-i4808e.pdf.

[11] MONRE (Ministry of Natural Resources and Environment), "Lao Environment Outlook 2012," Ministry of Natural Resources and Environment, Vientiane, Lao PDR, 2012, accessed April 26, 2019. https://data.opendevelopmentmekong.net/dataset/be0addb0-adfa-484c-88c2-32a9219db511/resource/9c1229cb-25e4-4cbb-be23-2121c0012a50/download/lao_eo_2012.pdf; USAID, "Drivers of Deforestation in the Greater Mekong Subregion: Lao PDR Country Report," USAID Lowering Emissions in Asia's Forests, 2015, accessed April 29, 2019. https://data.opendevelopmentmekong.net/lo/dataset/a7319336-89bb-4511-9c81-e5441c61f877/resource/8fe5a029-4b36-47e9-a0cc-6bef0e0f0bb2/download/lao-pdr-final-revised-nov2015.pdf.

[12] MAF (Ministry of Agriculture and Forestry), Environmental and Social Management Framework. Vientiane, Lao PDR: Lao PDR Agriculture Commercialization Project (LACP), Ministry of Agriculture and Forestry, 2017.

forest products, which sustain food and income for subsistence in rural areas. Overall, although there are a wide range of legislative documents of environmental protection including forest protection and agricultural expansion that have been put in place, the implementation of such documents remains limited, resulting in the dramatic decline of the percentage of forest covers.

Besides deforestation, Laos is facing a serious concern over clean soil and water resources. Since pursuing the implementation of the national development plan, it has promoted the modernization and commercialization of agriculture, which has become one of the primary strategies with good potential to foster economic development. In doing so, agricultural investment from overseas via land concessions and contract farming is being encouraged. Over the past years, contract farming, especially cultivation of crops such as maize, cassava, rubber, fruits, and vegetables in northern Laos has rapidly expanded. Nevertheless, there have been numerous cases in which contract farming companies failed to comply with regulations and environmental standards causing various environmental issues including soil degradation and water resource contamination. The case studies of banana contract farming in Oudomxay demonstrate that there have been soil and water contamination through the utilization of chemical fertilizers, herbicides, and other agricultural chemicals in large quantities on banana plantations, resulting in soil degradation and water contamination in the rivers.[13] Moreover, the illegal dumping of wastes such as plastic bags and other packaging that is coated with agricultural chemicals is also a serious issue. The local authorities/governments lack experience in advanced equipment and human resources related to assessing environmental impact and regulating the implications of environment including the implementation standard for agricultural investment. Generally, public management in environmental protection at local level lacks effectiveness.

---

[13] S. Higashi, "Impacts on Regional Land Use from Investment in Banana Contract Farming by Chinese Companies: Case Studies in Oudomxay Province, Northern Laos," Mekong Watch, accessed 30 April 2019. http://www.mekongwatch.org/PDF/BananaFarmingNorthernLaos-report.pdf.

In addition to agricultural impacts on environment, the mining industry is another point of concern. Having abundant mineral resources, the number of foreign direct investment has increased, which results in rapid economic growth. On the other hand, the operation of mining firms has polluted soil and water due to the use of chemicals, specifically cyanide. This has been dangerous for those living near the mining sites including animals as well as underwater living creatures. A study finds that the utilization of cyanide in gold mining in northern Laos has caused the death of fishes, other aquatic animals and soil contamination.[14] This also has harmfully affected the people in those polluted areas because they could not continue living as usual. Moreover, although larger-scale mining operations applied advanced technologies to the utilization of industrial chemicals more safely and efficiently, those operations had adversely impacted the environment by, for instance, degrading large areas of dense forest and destroying biodiversity.[15]

Apart from the limited paradigm of economic development concerned, individual (consumer) behavior is one of the central issues in terms of environmental protection. This is mainly attributed to rapid urbanization, demonstrated by the fact that the population migrating from rural areas to cities had risen by 40% between 2005 and 2015.[16] The urban expansion in association with consumer behaviors lacking the awareness for environmental sustainability has resulted in the rise of waste generation in the country, particularly in major cities like Vientiane, Savannakhet, and Pakse. Like most countries in the world, Laos has insatiable appetites, which is producing a mountain of waste. Recent evidence shows that Laos generates municipal solid waste

---

[14] PEI (Poverty-Environment Initiative), "Economic, Social and Environmental Impacts of Investments in Mining: Lao PDR Issues Brief," UNDP, 2010, accessed April 29, 2019. https://data.opendevelopmentmekong.net/dataset/479cd7f0-c4d2-4d47-a46c-74f60f055793/resource/bc80c3f2-a332-4fa2-a017-197d6abc579b/download/pei-brief-082010miningenglishd.pdf.

[15] *Ibid.*

[16] MAF (Ministry of Agriculture and Forestry), Environmental and Social Management Framework. Vientiane, Lao PDR: Lao PDR Agriculture Commercialization Project (LACP), Ministry of Agriculture and Forestry, 2017.

averaged about 0.70 kg per capita per day, which is higher than that in the neighboring countries such as Cambodia and Myanmar.[17] Beyond individual behaviors, community waste management in Laos is somehow ineffective. This is illustrated by the amount of garbage that has been disposed by burning or tossing in vacant spaces, drainage channels and rivers. Landfill is the main disposal method for solid waste, while open burning is also practiced. Currently, there is one main landfill site in Vientiane and 14 landfills out of 141 towns across the country.[18] Hazardous wastes like batteries have no proper measures to keep track of potential leachate into soil or underground water. The waste management has become the responsibility of households or communities, and public waste management lacks efficiency, especially in local areas.[19]

Challenges of Environmental Protection and Experiences in Policymaking and Implementation

Over the past decades, the issue of economic gains outweighing environmental costs has been a controversy. It is not easy to achieve a balance between them, specifically, it is challenging for most developing countries to deal with this issue. Laos's economic growth largely relies on natural resources through high flow of foreign direct investment. However, the management and the exploitation of the natural

[17] UN (United Nations), "Waste Management in ASEAN Countries: Summary Report," United Nations Environment Programme, Thailand, 2017, accessed May 5, 2019. https://wedocs.unep.org/bitstream/handle/20.500.11822/21134/waste_mgt_asean_summary.pdf?sequence=1&amp%3BisAllowed=.

[18] AF (Asia Foundation), "Love Laos: Keep it Clean," Inasia Weekly Insights and Analysis, 2017, accessed April 29, 2019. http://web.archive.org/web/20181001035630/https://asiafoundation.org/2017/04/19/love-laos-keep-clean/.

[19] GGGI (Global Green Growth Institute), "Solid Waste Management in Vientiane, Lao P.D.R: Situation Assessment and Opportunities for Waste to Resource," Global Green Growth Institute, Korea, 2018, accessed May 3, 2019. http://www.greengrowthknowledge.org/sites/default/files/downloads/best-practices/Solid_Waste%20Management_in_Vientiane_Lao_PDR%20_GGGI.pdf.

resources in multiple scenarios are being implemented in an unsustainable and environmentally unfriendly way, and this has resulted in harmful implications for the environment.[20] Although the current overall quality of environmental conditions in Laos remains at a good level compared to other countries in the region, particularly in biodiversity, human activities and the pace of economic development increasingly put pressure on environmental protection, and are challenging in the long run.

In recent years, an improvement of legislation relating to environmental protection toward sustainable economic development has been made. Nevertheless, there is a limited paradigm of economic development which lacks sustainability and inclusive environmental protection, ranging from natural resource management including forest, land, water resources to institutions and instruments, and public awareness and participation.[21] For instance, a recent strategy on national green growth, which is in line with the priorities under the eighth National Socio-Economic Development Plan (2016–2020), aims to deliver environmentally inclusive economic growth and also to reshape the development programs in a more sustainable manner. The strategy emphasizes the need to utilize the natural resources more effectively and efficiently, while taking a development path that is more resilient to risks including climate change.[22] One of the key strategies is the "polluter pays" principle, which means that the industries who produce pollution need to pay additional taxes. Currently, industries pay corporate tax, which is calculated at 24% of a company's profit, as well as its excise, value added and income tax.[23] Yet, little or

---

[20] MPI (Ministry of Planning and Investment), The 8th Five Year National Socio-Economic Development Plan (2016–2020). Vientiane, Lao PDR: Ministry of Planning and Investment, 2016.

[21] *Ibid.*

[22] World Bank, "Lao PDR's Green Growth Reforms get $40 Million Boost with Credit from World Bank," The World Bank IBRD-IDA, 2019, accessed 19 October 2019. https://www.worldbank.org/en/news/press-release/2019/05/28/lao-pdrs-green-growth-reforms-get-40-million-boost-with-credit-from-world-bank.

[23] PPP (Phnom Penh Post), "Lao Government Considers Tax To Protect Environment," The Phnom Penh Post, Cambodia, 2019, accessed May 2, 2019.

no specific plans or measures have been made, including the form of this new tax and how it would be implemented.[24] It is understandable that posing such a tax could discourage both domestic and foreign investments, hindering the economy growth, which is tricky to balance between the need for economic development and environmental protection. Also, it is comprehensible that there is a wide gap between the formulated strategies or policies and the implementation. These are common challenges faced by developing countries, not merely Laos.

Basically, Laos has formulated a wide range of legislations including laws, decrees, regulations, and guidelines for assessment and management of environmental impacts associated with development projects. The 2013 environmental protection law is likely to be the fundamental legislation regarding sustainable environmental protection. This law sets up a basic structure underlying a framework of integrated environmental resource management with the goal of sustainable utilization of natural resources. The law includes plans for the protection, improvement, mitigation, and restoration of the environment and guidelines for environmental management and assessment and monitoring. The Ministry of Natural Resources and Environment is in charge of implementing the law, while other ministries have issued guidelines for carrying out the law's provisions. However, as an LCD, more acute challenges have arisen in Laos largely due to the constraints of human and financing resources and the underlying limitations in detailed procedures and legislation including legal and institutional frameworks.

This can be noted by a variety of gaps between policymaking and implementation, specifically the procedures and the practices of the environmental impact assessment (EIA), which are ambiguous in terms of roles and responsibilities among public agencies and other stakeholders. The coordination among the EIA proponents such as consultants, relevant ministries, local authorities, and decision makers

---

https://aipasecretariat.org/lao-pdr-lao-government-considers-tax-to-protect-environment/.

[24] *Ibid.*

is somehow weak.[25] This leads not only to the dearth of scoping, impact assessment, and viewpoints in EIA documents but also affects the earlier stage of project development prior to obtaining EIA clearance.[26] Lacking coordination is not only confined to the delayed results in decision-making process but also impedes the effective implementation of environmental regulations. Consequently, most deficiencies in EIA systems can be attributed to the weak performance in all underlying measures. The measures basically aim to promote good practices, which underpin the successful application of systemic approaches. Nevertheless, their weak quality will adversely influence the effectiveness and robustness of EIA implementation and practices. Thus, the key challenge posed to implementation of monitoring activities is the deficiency of institutions that arises predominantly from the shortage of technical know-how or qualified officials and monitoring equipment and other necessary resources. In brief, the systems for implementing and monitoring environmental impacts are ineffective and inefficient.[27]

Furthermore, there is insufficient expertise among decision makers and public involvements. Lacking expertise has resulted in the weak enforcement of environmental legislation including the EIA regulations and poor monitoring programs. In most developed nations, multiple stakeholders' participation including the general public is engaged in various stages of EIA, especially in the decision-making process, while in the least developed countries, including Laos, the points raised from public are rarely considered in the

[25] JICA (Japan International Cooperation Agency), "Profile on Environmental and Social Considerations in Lao PDR," Japan International Cooperation Agency, Vientiane, Lao PDR, 2013, accessed April 30, 2019, http://open_jicareport.jica.go.jp/pdf/12144762.pdf.

[26] S. Wayakone and M. Inoue, "Evaluation of the Environmental Impacts Assessment (EIA) System in Lao PDR," *Journal of Environmental Protection* 3(12, 2012): 1655–1670.

[27] JICA (Japan International Cooperation Agency), "Profile on Environmental and Social Considerations in Lao PDR," Japan International Cooperation Agency, Vientiane, Lao PDR, 2013, accessed April 30, 2019, http://open_jicareport.jica.go.jp/pdf/12144762.pdf.

process of planning and decision-making. This is mainly because most of the policies are centrally made. This is why public engagement is limited for both domestic and international organizations. As a consequence, the effectiveness of public participation in the EIA system remains challenging, which needs the development of good guidelines for further public participation.

Recommendations to ASEAN Member Countries and China

While Laos is enjoying its economic growth mainly driven by the abundance of natural resources, public management in sustainable environmental protection is tested. In ASEAN, a wide range of documents related to collective collaboration on environmental protection have been put in place. However, the implementation of those documents within ASEAN has made little progress compared to other areas such as economic cooperation, which is widening and deepening. A study claims that the challenges posed by ASEAN are multiplied, and this includes unbalanced development between the economic community and building a community toward environmental sustainability, which is tricky to cope with.[28] Yet, the imperative action that all countries in the region including China need to take is transformative change, which requires not only the governments, but also the market including traders, manufacturers, consumers, financial/investment communities and other stakeholders to be sustainability-oriented.[29] If this kind of holistic change approach can be applied, it would be served as a more effective means of linking

---

[28] S. S. C. Tay, C. L. Chen and X. Y. Lau, "ASEAN Approaches to Environmental Protection and Sustainable Development Cooperating Across Borders, Sectors, and Pillars of Regional Community," Global Megatrends: Implications for the ASEAN Economic Community, Singapore Institute of International Affairs, 2017, accessed May 6, 2019. https://asean.org/storage/2017/09/Ch.4_ASEAN-Approaches-to-Environmental-Protection-and-Sustainable-Dev.pdf.

[29] *Ibid*; M. McGrath, "Nature Crisis: Humans Threaten 1 m Species with Extinction," Science and Environment, BBC, 2019, accessed May 6, 2019. https://www.bbc.com/news/science-environment-48169783.

economic development with environmental concerns by taking into account wider aspects of development including political, economic, social, and environmental dimensions through inclusive consultation and meaningful participation of multiple stakeholders. The following policy recommendations are the practical remedies ranging from national and regional levels to beyond.

Growth must be reframed for national and regional sustainability. This is the transformative change that needs to reframe decision-making to better reconcile economic growth with sustainable growth. In this region, the central environmental issues for the trans-boundary impacts of air and water pollution would be the haze, which mainly involves Indonesia, Malaysia, Brunei, Singapore, and Thailand, causing economic loss; the case of the Mekong conflicts on water resources management among Cambodia, Laos, Myanmar, Thailand, and Vietnam cause constraints on their relations. Thus, the economic merit can be contested against sustainable development.

As ASEAN is moving toward robust economic community building, the cluster of air, soil, and water resources is a crucial factor of production for regional economic development. Therefore, ASEAN needs to pay attention to managing trans-boundary impacts on the environment. The paradigm of collaboration on the environment in the European Union (EU) can be an interesting model for applying in ASEAN. The EU has made a deliberate attempt to harmonize or integrate the environmental standards and regulations throughout its members, which comprise both economic and environmental concerns. Furthermore, although ASEAN has not reached regional standards on environmental protection such as the EIA, the ASEAN members can learn from other regional cooperation efforts including the Asia-Pacific Economic Cooperation (APEC), which has non-binding framework on environmental sustainability. However, the APEC members have pledged that they will not lower environmental standards for economic advantage. Moreover, EU has experience in significantly addressing and minimizing environmental impacts by promoting economic incentives to firms that innovate environment-friendly technologies.

Given the paradigms, ASEAN needs a solid commitment to strengthening sustainable environmental protection in parallel with their economic development. The 2025 AEC Blueprint has underpinned sustainable economic development, yet the concrete and specific action plans are limited. To address the challenge, ASEAN members should not be merely confined to the environmental sector, the economic one needs to be involved in facilitating. Both environmental and economic sectors should collaborate closely to integrate economic growth with environmental sustainability. It should be compulsory for economic entities, particularly firms, to be socially and environmentally responsible. However, seeking practical remedies to integrate both of them throughout ASEAN would be tricky, partly due to the development gaps and the distinct differences in the capacities of individual ASEAN members' environmental authorities and policies as well as priorities. Therefore, ASEAN needs to pledge itself regarding the environmental sustainability in the region.

In addition, reframing growth for sustainability is also linked with the issue of institutions. Although recognizing the significance of environmental protection, several ASEAN members presented little institutional development for environmental collaboration. For instance, the mechanism of ASEAN coordinating council, which has a function to submit reports to the ASEAN leaders for their consideration. In practice, a number of issues including environmental concerns do not go beyond their talk-shop or discussion because economic and political concerns are more substantive, as a result, the environmental issue is likely to be dismissed.[30] To cope with this challenge, it would be effective for environmental issues to be better integrated at the national level by each ASEAN member prior to

[30] S. S. C. Tay, C. L. Chen and X. Y. Lau, "ASEAN Approaches to Environmental Protection and Sustainable Development: Cooperating Across Borders, Sectors, and Pillars of Regional Community," Global Megatrends: Implications for the ASEAN Economic Community, Singapore Institute of International Affairs, 2017, accessed May 6, 2019. https://asean.org/storage/2017/09/Ch.4_ASEAN-Approaches-to-Environmental-Protection-and-Sustainable-Dev.pdf.

raising the issue at regional level (unless the ASEAN leaders can see the significance of new economic paradigms such as renewable energy as an area of innovation and untapped the potential for future economic growth). This would lead to environmental concerns being intertwined with political and economic concerns, and have the potential for ASEAN to be pioneers in a future-oriented industry.

At present, when we look at different sectors of economies in each ASEAN member, it remains ambiguous how the issue of economic growth and sustainability is dealt with by national agencies. More specifically, the issues of environment and sustainability are frequently seen as a separated function with less power than economic factors or little influence over policies on economic development. This is likely to be the issue at regional level reflected at local and national levels in spite of a few attempts to synchronize economic growth and sustainability. The case of Singapore may be a good example for ASEAN members to examine, learn from, and put into practice. Singapore set up a national climate change coordination secretariat under the purview of the prime minister's office and the deputy prime minister is in charge as the head of this secretariat. The secretariat involves not only the environment minister but also ministers from trade and industry, national development, and other related ministries. This mechanism is attributed the success of Singapore as one of the world's leading countries in harmonizing economic growth with environmental sustainability. Furthermore, there are numerous successful initiatives that ASEAN members can learn from, such as the initiative of Indonesia regarding integrating financial regulations and policies with environmental sustainability. The initiative has wider implications on economic activities, which requires banks to screen credit and business risks that can arise from environmental and sustainability issues affecting other sectors. Given the attempts, the public and private agencies at the national level should collaborate closely, particularly in information and idea exchanges. In the past, there were a number of growth and sustainability dialogues in ASEAN. However, most private sectors were not invited to the conferences. For instance, the green farming projects, for which each central bank of ASEAN has discussed sharing information and views about green farming techniques, lack in inclusive views and responses. Thus, it would be better if the private sectors could have their views on the issues. Therefore enhancing coordination and collaboration at national and regional levels, and between public and private sectors is necessary. In that sense, there should be a specific mechanism that can be in charge of the matter.

Apart from cooperation at national and regional levels, strengthening ASEAN's partnerships is a crucial means of improving environmental sustainability and China is an integral part of such sustainability. Each national government in ASEAN is looking at sustainability issues in the global context. In recent years, the issues of growth and sustainability, including environmental protection, have been developed and strengthened by the UN's efforts of describing and identifying issues in the context of SDGs and the Paris Agreement on Climate Change. All ASEAN members have participated in these processes and have agreed to report on their actions. Given the global agreements and national obligations, ASEAN could take up a position of leading a new paradigm of economic growth around the globe. However, ASEAN members have not been able to achieve this ambition because of their difficulties in policies, priorities and institutions. Thus, China as a core engine of global economic growth with experiences in green city development should share information and facilitate ASEAN members to seek a path toward environmental sustainability. For example, China should provide economic assistance relating to the paradigm shifts regarding carbon and other gases such as energy production and other technological transfer that are minimizing climate change. Likewise, China should support the initiatives of ASEAN regarding the green economic growth such as ASEAN smart cities network. There are 26 major cities across the region participating in the pilot projects and ASEAN needs funds to implement such an initiative. Furthermore, China should promote ASEAN in strengthening their institutions on the issue of environmental transparency. The implementation of regulations or policies would be ineffective if there is no transparency, for example, the issue in reporting the outcomes of EIA and other environmental standards.

By 2030, ASEAN has set a goal of becoming a borderless economic community. At present, the progress of its economic integration is on track to widen and deepen, however, there is a need to identify issues and respond to challenges to seek collective remedies by ASEAN and its strategic partnerships including China, which will increase productivity. The widening development gap among ASEAN members remains challenging. Cambodia, Laos, and Myanmar are regarded as the less developed countries in the region. This explains why promoting environmental protection in parallel with economic growth is not easy to achieve. Laos, as discussed earlier, has various difficulties in the implementation of environmental protection including the constraints of human resource/environmental expertise, promoting public awareness on environmental values, and managing waste in an efficient manner. Therefore, providing assistance including technical knowledge, capacity building in institutions, and application of advanced science and technologies will facilitate these countries to better catch up with other ASEAN members and enhance the environmental sustainability in the region.

With growing campaigns of climate change, the paradigm of economic development across the globe is no longer a concern of economic growth. The green growth for sustainable development, including the SDGs and the Paris Agreement, is increasingly becoming a central issue for not only the national government but also regional and global organizations. In ASEAN, environmental concerns over air and water resources are evident these days. These concerns of local and transboundary pollution will impact the economic development including the livelihoods of millions of dwellers across the region. Therefore, reconciling both growth and sustainability is vital. This requires better environmental protection, which is not simple and otherwise might have devastating environmental impacts on human well-being and all forms of lives. Yet, the attempts can be made not only by ASEAN individually and collectively, but beyond the region, China and other actors should not be excluded. As a good attempt, ASEAN and China should closely collaborate at all levels of governance at national and regional levels, specifically between the governments and private sectors. The economic paradigm of EU in promoting economic incentives and making firms innovate environment-friendly technologies is not redundant.

Conclusion

In summary, Laos's pressing issues around environmental sustainability range from restrained individual awareness to weak public management resulting in forest degradation and soil and water deterioration. These concerns are being driven by the growth-led strategies including industrialization and commercialization within a limited paradigm of economic development. To address the challenges, natural resources need to be managed more effectively with less or no waste. In doing so, it is imperative to strengthen the enforcement of environment-related laws and regulations, build the capacity of central and local institutions, and raise public awareness on values of environmental sustainability. Policymaking and approaches need to be more open and inclusive. Beyond the national level, ASEAN as an intergovernmental organization is an integral part of helping Laos to carry out sustainable environmental protection. Furthermore, close collaboration within ASEAN members and between ASEAN and other partners including China, specifically cooperation between economic and environmental sectors as well as public and private sectors, is imperative for joint policy formulation and implementation if a sustainable and inclusive community of green economic growth needs to be achieved.

https://doi.org/10.1142/9789811225222_0007

Chapter 7

The Cooperation between Myanmar and China in Oil and Gas Sector since 1988

Daw Thida

Myanmar Institute of Strategic and International Studies (MISIS), Myanmar

Introduction

As energy utilization has brought economic boost and social development, both the developed and developing countries have shifted their focus from geo-politics to geo-economy, trying to expand access to energy for their economic growth. Therefore, access to cheap energy has become essential to well-functioned modern economies. Under such conditions, the resource-rich countries have become important on the political stage and Myanmar is of no exception. Many energy-thrusting countries try to cooperate with these resource-rich countries in the oil and gas sector. Despite the status of the top five energy exporters in the region, Myanmar is insufficient in terms of domestic energy consumption, which has demotivated successive governments from taking further efforts. Therefore, studying its energy exports and how they affect the development of the country is of necessity. This chapter will mainly focus on Myanmar's oil and gas exports to her neighboring country, China, which, as one of the world's most populous countries, is a fast-growing economy with world-class energy consumption and production. In China's pursuit of regional economic, political, and social stability, Myanmar is geopolitically significant to China given its access to the Indian Ocean and its extensive natural resources. Moreover, Myanmar also plays a strategic role in the 21st-Century Maritime Silk Road. Its natural gas resources and strategic location bordering Indian Ocean can help China import oil directly from the Middle East, South America, and Africa while avoiding the dangerous Straits of Malacca.

The Needs for Development in Myanmar's Energy Sector

Myanmar is rich in natural resources, namely crude oil, natural gas, hydroelectricity, biomass, and coal. There are 17 geological sedimentary basins identified in Myanmar, of which six have been on full-scale production. The country also has a total of 20 gas-fired power plants.

However, Myanmar's oil and gas industry is restrained by technical limitations and government's reluctance to accept foreign investment until the State Law and Order Restoration Council (SLORC) took power in September 1988. SLORC opened up the opportunity for foreign companies to explore oil and gas. In addition, the centrally planned economy was shifted to a market-oriented economy. With the adoption of the market-oriented economy in the late 1980s, the government formulated 12 economic, social, and political objectives, which invited technical know-how and investments from home and abroad. With this aim, the Union of Myanmar Foreign Investment Law (FIL) was promulgated on 30 November 1988. The basic principles of the FIL are promotion and expansion of exports and exploitation of natural resources.[1]

Myanmar broadened the energy sector by inviting foreign technicians and investment. In the past, Myanmar Oil and Gas Enterprise

[1] The New Light of Myanmar, July 6, 1995, p. 1.

(MOGE, formed in 1963) was a sole operator of oil and gas exploration and production as well as domestic gas transmission. Myanmar is divided into gas production blocks for the purpose of managing exploration and drilling activities. There are 104 blocks demarcated both onshore and offshore (GC) for conducting petroleum-related operations as can be seen in Figure 1.[2]

Since 9 October 1989, Myanmar has issued exploration licenses to multinational oil and gas companies. Among them, China, India, and Thailand are the top three investors, by signing the Production Sharing Contract (PSC) for allocation of the existing wells, Improved Petroleum Recovery (IPR) contracts for improving the production in existing wells, and Production Compensation Contracts (PCC) for early monetization of petroleum resources of Myanmar. The most common form of contract signed by the International Oil Company (NOC) in Myanmar is the PSC.

The Energy Need for the Economic Development of China

China is the world's second largest energy consumer, only after the United States. Residential and transport energy efficiency is important to China and its NOCs have huge impact on the whole energy sector.[3]

In pursuit of the multi-pronged strategy, China has endorsed overseas equity investment and entered a range of contracts with various foreign nations. The three largest NOCs, China National Petroleum Corporation (CNPC) (1988), China Petrochemical Corporation (predecessor of SINOPEC), and China National Offshore Oil Corporation (CNOOC) (1982), were established during the phase of energy institution reform. All of them are running in Myanmar's oil and gas sector.

---

[2] U Zaw Aung, Overview of Oil and Gas Sector in Myanmar. Naypyitaw: Energy Planning Department, 2013, pp. 2–3.

[3] David Steinberg and Fan Hongwei, Modern China–Myanmar Relations, a Dilemma of Mutual Dependence. Thailand: Nordic Institute of Asian Studies, 2012, p. 180.

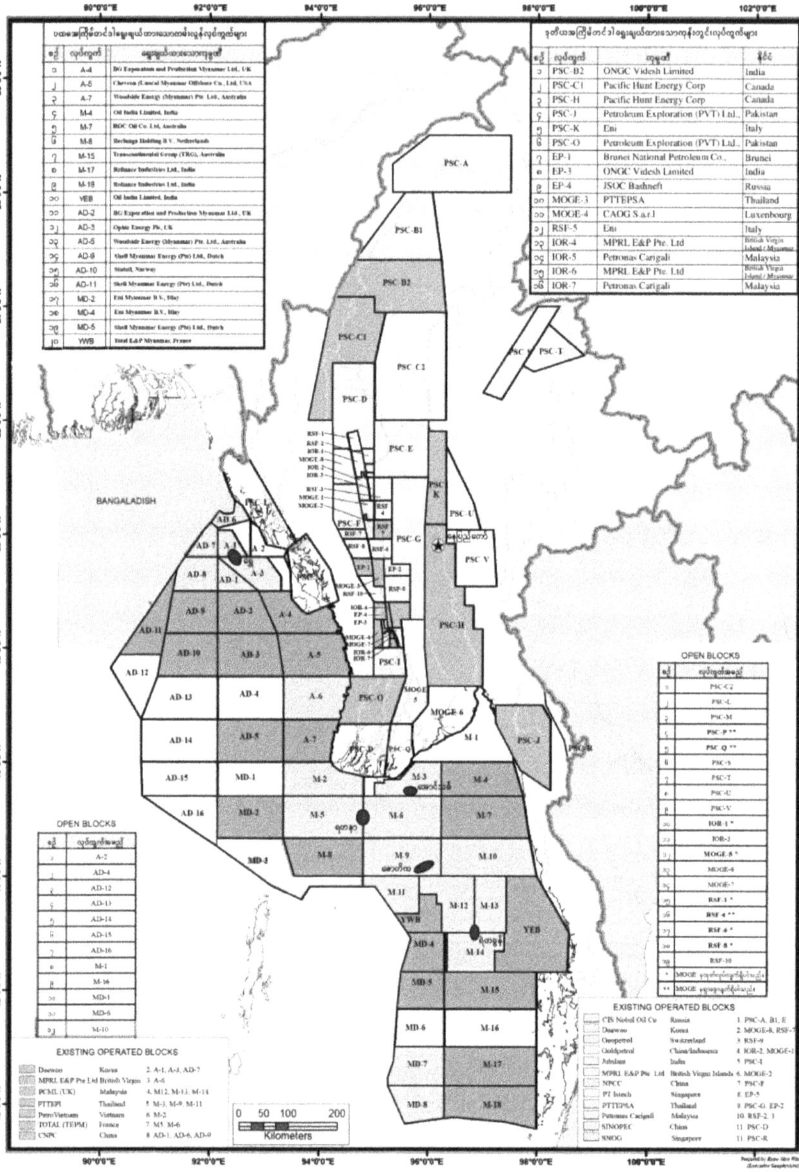

Figure 1 Offshore and Onshore Gas Blocks in Myanmar

Source: https://www.moee.gov.mm/en/ignite/page/145.

However, the more the economy develops, the greater the amount of domestic oil consumed, thus energy is under surging demand. Chinese energy demand has rapidly increased between 9% and 10% each year.[4] In 1993, China became a net importer of crude oil with approximately 40% of the world's oil demand.[5] Therefore, China embarked on a "Go-Out" policy to procure energy assets in July 1994.[6] In late 1995, the government launched "grasp the large and release the small" policy, which aimed to make several hundred large state-owned enterprises (SOEs) into world-class businesses. During 1996–2000, the oil and gas industries were also restructured and China launched its "West Development" campaign to bridge the gap between the economies along its eastern coastal regions and its western ones by helping them with oil and gas industry building.

After its entry in the World Trade Organization (WTO) in December 2001, new amendments to the principal regulations governing foreign participation in onshore and offshore upstream petroleum projects had brought regulations in line with China's WTO commitments. Government encouraged the "construction and operation of oil and gas pipelines" in the western provinces by foreign enterprises.

Chinese market had relied on the global energy market during 1990–2011. Furthermore, the amount of imported natural gas production also increased from 43.3 to 94.9 billion cubic feet (according to Energy Information Administration). In late 2011, the national "Bridgehead Strategy" was launched which aimed to turn Yunnan into a strategic corridor and a bridgehead for China's strategic engagement in the Indian Ocean.[7]

---

[4] Yu Bao and Gordon Houlden, The Evolution of China's Energy Institutions: Centralization Versus Decentralization. Canada: China Institute University of Alberta Edmonton, 2001, p. 64.

[5] Tju Liang Chua and Ashleigh Au, Upstream Oil and Gas in China, China, Doing Business in China. Huntington: Juris Publishing, 2009, pp. 5, 8.

[6] Jimin Zhao, Reform of China's Energy Institutions and Policies: Historical Evolution and Current Challenges. Harvard: Harvard University Press, 2001, p. 90.

[7] Namrata Panwar, India and China Competing over Myanmar Energy. Leicester: Working draft for BISA Conference, 2009, pp. 5–6.

China had not shown much concern about energy security until 1993 after the transition from being an oil exporter to a net oil importing country.[8] It made China's external sources of energy important to support its industrializing economy. Although the Chinese government had promoted energy conservation and accelerated the supply of energy through the use of market mechanisms, it still depended on oil from the Middle East.[9]

Asia-Pacific has two significant sea lanes of communication, one passing through the South China Sea to the Indian Ocean and the Middle East, the other passing through East China and the Sea of Japan to the Pacific Ocean and the Pacific coast of the US and Canada. The South China Sea provides shipping routes connecting Northwest Asia with Southeast Asia and the Middle East. Since there was no way for the Chinese navy to protect the long sea route from the Middle East through the Indian Ocean and the South China Sea, China's physical distance and presence of Western oil companies had made difficulties for China to gain secured possession over oil and gas fields. Therefore, the primary objective of China's supply diversification strategy was to reduce dependence on oil from the Persian Gulf.

Access to Myanmar's ports and overland transportation routes through Myanmar was seen as vital to China. This access would be able to shorten the distance by 3,000 km by avoiding the Straits of Malacca.[10] Furthermore, the Sino-Myanmar oil pipeline would reduce by over 1,820 sea miles the journey to Guangzhou (City of China) from the Middle East.[11] In terms of transportation, Myanmar is also the only passage for Yunnan to reach South Asia and an important gateway to the Indian Ocean.

---

[8] David Blumental, Tju Liang Chua and Ashleigh Au, "Upstream Oil and Gas in China," in Doing Business In China, ed. Michael J. Moser and Fu Yu (Huntington: Juris Publishing, 2020).

[9] *Ibid.*, p. 14.

[10] Tuli Sinha, China–Myanmar Energy Engagements, Challenges and Opportunities for India. IPCS Brief No. 134, 2009, pp. 1–2.

[11] David Steinberg and Fan Hongwei, Modern China–Myanmar Relations, a Dilemma of Mutual Dependence. Thailand: Nordic Institute of Asian Studies, 2012, pp. 170–171.

Myanmar is crucial not only for China's energy needs but also for international cooperation in oil and gas sector.[12] From then on, China's enterprises have gradually expanded their investments in Myanmar's industrial infrastructure.[13] In cooperation with Myanmar, China aimed at the three main fields: infrastructure development, supporting State-Owned Economic Enterprises (SEEs) and energy exploration.

The Cooperation between Myanmar and China in Oil and Gas Sector

Myanmar and China share a common history of colonialism and have strong economic ties. China is the largest investor and trading partner of Myanmar. When State Peace and Development Council (SPDC, former SLORC) opened up Myanmar to foreign economic investment, China stepped into the vacuum that was created by Western sanctions and compensated for Myanmar's need for trade and economic cooperation.

The Chinese side focused on infrastructure development. Many projects were constructed by China, which include the Letpadaung copper mines at Monywa in northwest Myanmar and the Myitsone dam, a 6,000 MW capacity hydropower plant, at the confluence of the Maykha and Malikha rivers, which forms the source of the Irrawaddy River and the oil and gas pipelines.[14]

When China began to seek new resources and markets in Myanmar in 2000, the two countries expanded their cooperation. In 2001, Chinese enterprises got involved in Myanmar oil and gas explorations.[15] The most significant China–Myanmar energy cooperation is

---

[12] Tuli Sinha, China–Myanmar Energy Engagements, Challenges and Opportunities for India. IPCS Brief No. 134, 2009, pp. 1–2.

[13] Isabel Hilton, China in Myanmar: Implications for the future, The Norwegian Peacebuilding Resource Centre (NOREF) Report, October 2013, pp. 1–2, https://www.files.ethz.ch/isn/172094/822f00b4d7da6439a3252789b404f006.pdf.

[14] Chinese Involvement in Myanmar's Energy Sector, p. 71. www.http://ics.um.edu.my.

[15] Lixin Geng, Sino-Myanmar Relations: Analysis and Prospects Australia. Bond: ePublications, 2007, p. 1.

the oil and gas pipelines which started in 2009.[16] CNOCs, CNPC and CNOOC started oil exploration projects and competed with other countries including India and South Korea to secure access to new gas fields and potential reserves of gas off the west coast.[17] The two pipelines are important components of China's ability to deliver oil and gas to southwest China. The Chinese companies in Myanmar's oil and gas sector are listed in Table 1.

In the cooperation between Myanmar and China in oil and gas sector, the main offshore gas fields are Shwe Gas Fields (A-1, A-3), A-4, M-10, AD-1, AD-6, AD-8, and AD-7 that can be seen in Table 2. Among them, Shwe natural gas field is the main field of Myanmar and China cooperation. It is a project of the MOGE. South Korea based Daewoo International is the largest stakeholder in the consortium (51%). The remaining is divided into the state-owned Korean Gas Corporation (8%), India's state-owned Oil and Natural Gas Corporation (ONGC) (17%), MOGE (15%) and the Gas Authority of India Ltd. (GAIL) (9%). These consist of three independent gas discoveries, the Shwe gas field, Shwe Phyu gas field, and Mya gas field.

These deposits are collectively one of the world's largest, holding an estimated 12 trillion cubic feet (tcf) of gas. China cooperated in exploration, production, and transportation.[18]

The Shwe, Shwe Phyu Fields (Block A-1), and Mya Field (Block A-3)

The Shwe and Shwe Phyu fields (Block A-1) are parts of the Shwe fields. A-1 block was found in 2000. Daewoo is the majority owner and operator of the blocks. Daewoo had brought in a number of minority partners for the gas fields. It produced 32 mmscfd and more amount of natural

[16]Tenzing Chopel Sherpa, Importance of Myanmar in China's Strategic Interest: A Case Study on Sino-Myanmar Oil and Gas Pipelines. Gangtok: Sikkim University, 2016, p. 7.
[17]Zhao Hong, "China–Myanmar Energy Cooperation and Its Regional Implications," *Journal of Current Southeast Asian Affairs* 30(4, 2011), p. 92.
[18]MOGE, MOEE (Naypyitaw: September 2017).

Table 1 China's cooperation in Myanmar's oil and gas sector

No	Year	Company	Country	Name of the Project	Field/Block	Location	J/V (%) Sharing
1.	2004	(1) Daewoo International	S. Korea	Shwe Gas	Shwe, Shwe Phyu,	Rakhine State	51
		(2) State-owned Korean Gas Corporation	S. Korea	Project	Mya (Block		8
		(3) ONGC	India	(offshore)	A-1, A-3)		17
		(4) MOGE	Myanmar				15
		(5) GAIL	India				9
2.	2004	(1) SINOPC	China		Block A-4	Rakhine State	80
		(2) MOGE	Myanmar		Bock M-10	Mottama	20
3.		(1) CNPC	China	Shwe Gas	Blocks		80
		(2) MOGE	Myanmar	Project	(AD-1	Rakhine State	20
				(offshore)	AD-6		
					AD-8)		
4.	2007	(1) CNPC	China	(onshore)	Blocks	Tuyintaung	
					RSF-2	Gwegyo-Ngashandang	
					RSF-3	Tetma	
					(IOR-3,	Indaw-Yeman	
					IOR-4)	Shwebo-Monywa	
					C-1		
					C-2		
5.	2007	(1)CNOOC	China	(onshore)	Block-D	Sagaing and Magwe Divisions	
6.	2007	SINOPEC	China	offshore	Blocks (M-2, M-3, M-4, M-10)	Mottama	
7.	2007		China	offshore	AD-7	Rakhine State	

Sources: MOGE, MOEE, Naypyitaw, September 2017.

Table 2 Offshore blocks with China in Myanmar

Block	Block A-1	Block A-3	Block A-4	Block M-10	Blocks AD-1, AD-6, AD-8	Block AD-7
Location	Offshore Rakhine	Offshore Rakhine	Offshore Rakhine	Offshore Mottama	Offshore Rakhine	Offshore Rakhine
Basin	Bengal Basin	Bengal Basin	Bengal Basin	Bengal Basin	Bengal Basin	Bengal Basin
Size	2,119 sqkm		2,889 sqkm	5,320 sqkm		1,684 sqkm
Contract	Production Sharing Contract (PSC)	4,907 sqkm	Production Sharing Contract (PSC)	Production Sharing Contract (PSC)	Production Sharing Contract (PSC)	Production Sharing Contract (PSC)
Signing Date	4 August 2008	18 February 2008	14 December 2004	14 December 2004	15 January 2007	February 2007
Duration of Contract	30 years	30 years	30 years	30 years	30 years	30 years

Sources: MOGE, MOEE, Naypyitaw, September 2017.

gas was expected.[19] Therefore, China cooperated in A-1 gas exploration sector and the China Petroleum & Chemical Corporation (SINOPEC), the DianQuan-Gui Petroleum Exploration Bureau of China, and the MOGE signed a PSC in September 2004 for exploration.

Both countries invested $30 million for exploration. They agreed on the two PSCs at offshore Block A-4 (Rakhine State) and offshore Block M-10 (Mottama) with areas of 2,889 square miles and 5,320 square miles, respectively, on 14 December 2004.[20] In late 2005, Myanmar signed a Memorandum of Understanding (MoU) to sell 6.5 tcf of natural gas to China, setting the stage for a pipeline from the A-1 gas block in offshore Rakhine to Yunnan province.[21] Block A-3 was found on 18 February 2004. The A-1 and A-3 fields were expected to produce up to 10 tcf of gas over the next 30 years.[22] Duration of contracts with China was 30 years.

Another offshore block AD-7 was discovered in February 2007 at North West of Myanmar. Its acreage is 1,684 square kilometers. The Daewoo International is 100% operator. The CNPC and its subsidiary Chinnery Assets had also been awarded contracts to upgrade the four old oil fields in Central Myanmar. These companies had invested $16.3 million, rather small compared to the $2,635 million total foreign investments in Myanmar's oil and gas sector. Myanmar–China cooperation on oil and gas sectors had been strengthened.[23]

Although Myanmar government received numerous offers to purchase gas from the Shwe fields, Myanmar accepted China's offer only in June 2008, and agreed to export 6.5 tcf of natural gas to China for

[19] Tenzing Chopel Sherpa, Importance of Myanmar in China's Strategic Interest: A Case Study on Sino-Myanmar Oil and Gas Pipelines. Gangtok: Sikkim University, 2016, p. 24.

[20] Xiaghui Zhu, Do the Myanmar–China Pipelines Put Myanmar at Risk? China: Institute of Southeast Asian Studies, Yunnan University, 2011, p. 3.

[21] Sun Yun, "China' Strategic Misjudgments on Myanmar," *Journal of Current Southeast Asian Affairs* 1(2012): pp. 83–84.

[22] MOGE, MOEE (Naypyitaw, September 2017), p. 1.

[23] Matthew Smith and Naing Htoo, Gas Politics: Shwe Gas Development in Burma, Watershed, Vol. 11, No. 2, November 2005–June 2006, https://earthrights.org/wp-content/uploads/gas-politics-shwe-gas-development-in burma.pdf.

over 30 years.[24] In 2008, Myanmar and China signed an agreement to sell natural gas from A-1 and A-3 blocks to China via pipelines. In addition, on 26 March 2009, China and Myanmar signed an agreement for the joint construction of $1.5 billion crude oil and $1.04 natural gas pipelines. Again on 16 June 2009, a Memorandum of Understanding for the Myanmar–China Oil Pipeline was signed in Beijing between Myanmar's Ministry of Energy and CNPC.

Shwe Gas Field's Production, Export, and Sales to China

The Shwe gas project production had increased from year to year. The wellhead production was 20,177.30 mmscfd, the amount of export was 16,030.57 mmscfd and the domestically used gas was 336.11 mmscfd in 2013.[25] In June 2017, the natural gas production was 831883.58 mmscfd and the total gas production from 2013 to June 2017 was 575,254.11 mmscfd. The total amount of exported gas was 501,940.91 mmscfd.

For exportation, only Shwe export gas sales increased during the period of 2013–2014 to 2015–2016 according to Table 3. However, the total amount of Myanmar gas sales was lower than 2015–2016.

China not only explores Myanmar's oil and gas sector but also transports required gas through pipelines. Myanmar–China oil and gas pipelines run in parallel and start near Kyaukpyu, Rakhine, on the west coast of Myanmar, where an oil terminal was constructed. The crude oil pipeline begins at Maday Island, whereas the gas pipeline begins at Ramree Island in Kyaukpyu. The pipelines are about 2,500 km long, with over 770 km (480 miles) laid in Myanmar's territory. The gas pipeline is 2,520 km long including the 793 km in Myanmar and the 1,727 km in China. According to Figure 2, the pipelines run through the Rakhine, Mandalay, Lashio, and Muse in Myanmar.[26]

[24] Zhao Hong, "China–Myanmar Energy Cooperation and Its Regional Implications," *Journal of Current Southeast Asian Affairs* 30(4, 2011), p. 93.

[25] MOGE, MOEE (Naypyitaw: September, 2017), p. 1.

[26] Tenzing Chopel Sherpa, Importance of Myanmar in China's Strategic Interest: A Case Study on Sino-Myanmar Oil and Gas Pipelines. Gangtok: Sikkim University, 2016, p. 11.

Table 3 Total income of Shwe export gas sales (financial year wise)

Month/ Year	INV. No. & Date	Domestic Gas		Export Gas		Total Myanmar Income ($)
		MMSCFD	MMBTU	MMSCFD	MMBTU	
2013–2014				37,040.58716	37,473,464.10414	109,239,917.06
2014–2015				128,135.41847	129,567,372.98645	351,953,056.33
2015–2016				163,806.51592	165,667,330.08597	326,604,214.28
2016–2017		27,915.49538	28,228,498.22221	157,077.35154	158,840,528.26891	220,191,555.54

Source: Shwe export gas sales (financial year wise), MOGE, MOEE, Naypyitaw, September 2017.

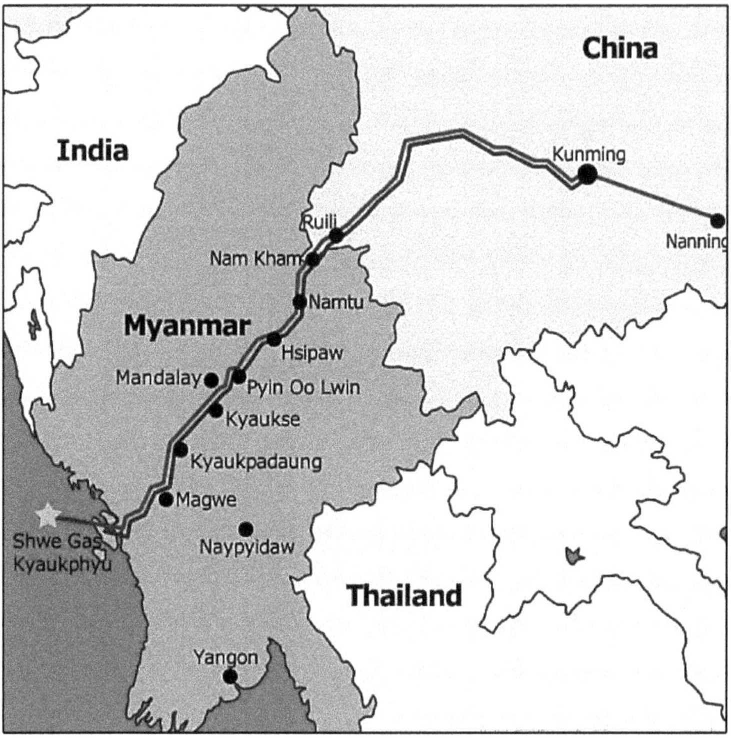

Figure 2 Sino-Myanmar Oil and Gas Pipelines

Source: Briefer on Chinese Investments in Myanmar, Ministry of National Planning and Economy of Myanmar, Yangon, January 3, 2014.

Then, the gas pipeline runs through Guizhou, Chongqing, and Guangxi in China. Finally, the pipelines end at Kunming, the capital city of Yunnan Province. One of the pipelines transports gas from Myanmar and the crude oil pipeline carries the crude oil that CNPC imports from Africa and the Middle East into China via Myanmar.

Shwe Project's partners are collectively known as the "Shwe Consortium". In 2009, CNPC's subsidiary, Southeast Asia Crude Pipeline Company, was assigned for designing, constructing, operating, and maintaining the crude oil and gas pipelines. The pipelines' construction on the Myanmar section began in June 2010 and started on the Chinese section about three months later. In addition, a 300,000-t crude oil wharf in Beijing and the 650,000 m^2 reservoirs at Maday Island in Rakhine for storage of water were built for the Myanmar–China pipelines. The reservoir is the main source of water for the pipeline operation. The Shwe consortium also operated an offshore pipeline for transporting crude oil and natural gas from Daewoo International's offshore blocks A-1 and A-3 in Myanmar to China. The Myanmar–China pipelines comprise multiple separate projects, each with distinct contracts and ownership structures.

The overland Shwe gas pipeline began at the offshore pipeline natural gas terminal and extended to the border with China's Yunnan province. The gas pipeline allowed delivery of natural gas from Myanmar's offshore fields to China with an annual capacity of up to 12 billion cubic meters of natural gas.[27] It was completed on 12 June 2013 and started to transport gas to China on 21 October 2013. Myanmar got 20% of the gas from the pipeline. The average total revenue for natural gas export from Myanmar to China is $31.066 billion for 30 years (2013–2043).[28]

With China's assistance, an oil refinery factory with the capacity of 56,000 barrels per day was constructed in Myotha, Mandalay Region. An agreement between China and Myanmar in oil and gas sector provided import of overseas oil via the Bay of Bengal and pumping it through the pipeline to supply a new 260,000 billion barrels per day (bpd) refinery in landlocked Yunnan province.[29] The 2,389 km long oil pipeline carried 22 million tons of crude oil per year from the Middle East and Africa to China. In addition, China has been transporting oil from the Maday Island to Southwest China through underground pipelines since 2016.[30] Myanmar got transit fees from China for oil transportation to China, the payment for the right of way, and the income tax for the transit fees got by the pipeline companies.[31]

---

[27] *Ibid*., p. 12.

[28] MOGE Financing Table, MOGE, MOEE (Naypyitaw, 2012).

[29] Crude oil transit trade licenses permission of and the actual imported conditions, National Planning and Economic Development (Ministry of Minister's Office: October, 2017), p. 23.

[30] Aung Yanma, "Local Fishermen Faced Difficulties at the Maday Deep Sea Port," *Daily Eleven Journal* (2017), pp. 1, 15.

[31] An Interview with U Kyaw Zeya, Deputy Director (Law), PSC Management Committee Office, Planning Department (Naypyitaw, Myanmar: October, 2017).

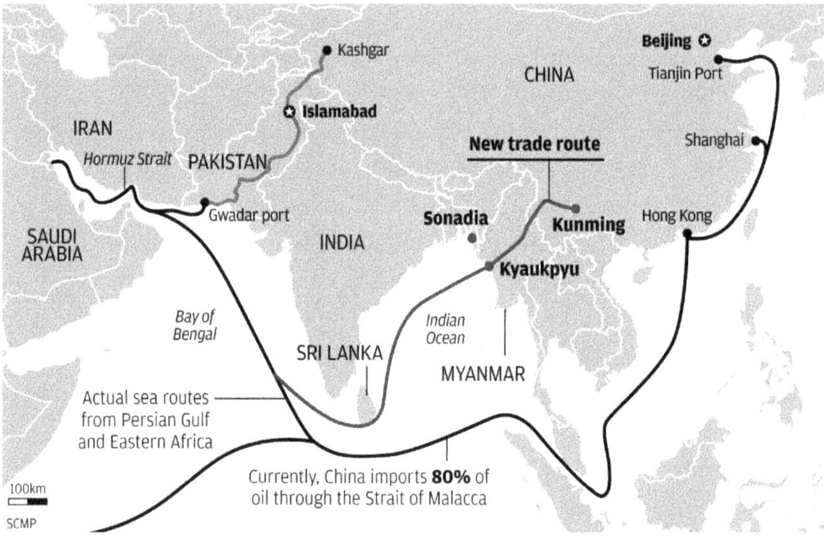

Figure 3 Oil Routes of China

Source: https://www.researchgate.net/figure/Chinese-oil-supply-chain-network-under-OBOR-Source-Adapted-from-Sheu-and-Kundu-8_fig3_324649303.

Sino-Myanmar Oil and Gas Pipeline

Sino-Myanmar pipeline is the fourth most important energy transportation route after the Central Asia pipelines (Kazakhstan–China oil pipeline and Turkmenistan–China gas pipeline), sea transportation and the Sino-Russia pipeline. The pipelines lie underneath, stretching 800 kilometers, or about 500 miles, from the Indian Ocean in the south — where the oil and gas will be loaded to the Chinese border in the north. It reaches Kunming via Mandalay and Muse. Through Kunming, it has direct linkages with major cities in China. By cooperation with Myanmar, China mitigated its dependence on the Malacca Straits for most of its oil imports from North Africa and the Middle East that can be seen in Figure 3.

Moreover, China has also built a gas reserve base and a wharf for oil tankers near Kyaukpyu in Rakhine State, marking the opening of a new oil trading route. The new oil gateway fitted with China's Belt and Road initiative (proposed in 2013), linking it with

Central Asia and Europe, also provided a direct alternative route to transport Middle Eastern oil via the Malacca Straits and Singapore.[32] China's coastal line is on the east side, leading naturally to the strategic prioritization of the Pacific. For inland China, however, it is more convenient and active to use the Indian Ocean as the outlet. The bridgehead strategy can bring enormous advantages to China with a long-term strategy to promote connectivity and cooperation between Myanmar and China. In addition, it can also provide one of Myanmar's energy sector's needs, the foreign direct investment (FDI).

China sought to raise natural gas imports via pipelines as natural gas use in China had also increased rapidly; China accounted for more than one-fourth of the global oil consumption growth in 2015.[33] On 30 April 2017, the amount of China's FDI in Myanmar's oil and gas sector was $2695.579 million.[34] The production of Shwe natural gas fields, the main field of Myanmar and China energy cooperation, was increased from 2013 to June 2017. The project made a tremendous contribution to the Myanmar economy not only by the influx of a huge investment into the country but also by the benefits acquired through the gas sales throughout the term of the project.[35]

The Impacts of Energy Cooperation between Myanmar and China

The energy cooperation between Myanmar and China was to link up the logistic system between the two countries. From an

---

[32] Myanmar–China Oil Pipeline Near Start-Up, Reuters, 3, https://www.forbes.com>2015/02/09.

[33] China International, Analysis, US Energy Information Administration (EIA) April 12, 2016, p. 5. https://www.eia.gov/beta/international/analysis.cfm?iso=CHN.

[34] Yearly Approved Amount of Foreign Direct Investment (by country), DICA, Yangon, 2017, p. 12.

[35] Han Muyar Win Shwe, Cooperative Social Responsibility Practices of Shwe Gas Project by Daewoo International Corporation, Yangon (MA Thesis, January, 2013), p. 30.

economic point of view, it brought many development opportunities not only for China but also for Myanmar.[36] Myanmar's oil and gas projects fueled much of Myanmar's economic growth. Since China had invested in Myanmar's oil and gas sector since 2004, China's investment rose from $20.18 million in 2004 to more than $1946.75 million in 2010, an increase of 9.542% in six years. According to the Myanmar Investment Commission, China invested about $13.6 billion in Myanmar, mostly in the energy sector, in the 2010–2011 financial years.[37] The sale of natural gas was the largest single income for Myanmar, accounting for nearly 50% of export revenues in 2008–2009.[38] Cheap fuel cost can save the user income and also reduce Myanmar's trade deficit with China. In addition, the China Development Bank and the Import–Export Bank provided $4.2 billion of interest-free loans to Myanmar for the construction of the pipelines and other major infrastructures.[39] Therefore, Myanmar received better energy development by exporting natural gas to China. CNPC had donated $12.5 million for construction of 44 schools, 24 health clinics, and other projects.

The pipelines' construction brought employment opportunities to 10,000 people, a large number of engineering and technical personnel trainees, and also promoted the development of tourism in Myanmar.[40] Therefore, Myanmar's economy improved through oil and gas cooperation with China. Moreover, the pipelines' construction particularly enhanced Myanmar's reputation as an oil and

---

[36] Tenzing Chopel Sherpa, Importance of Myanmar in China's Strategic Interest: A Case Study on Sino-Myanmar Oil and Gas Pipelines. Gangtok: Sikkim University, 2016, p. 62.

[37] Lixin Geng, Sino-Myanmar Relations: Analysis and Prospects Australia. Bond: ePublications, 2007, p. 5.

[38] Jacob Gronholt-Pedersen, "Myanmar Pipelines to Benefit China," *Asia News*, May 12, 2013, p. 2.

[39] Tenzing Chopel Sherpa, Importance of Myanmar in China's Strategic Interest: A Case Study on Sino-Myanmar Oil and Gas Pipelines. Gangtok: Sikkim University, 2016, p. 64.

[40] Jacob Gronholt-Pedersen, "Myanmar Pipelines to Benefit China," *Asia News*, May 12, 2013, p. 3.

gas producer which spurred greater investment in the energy sector.[41]

China benefited by not only opting for a convenient alternative to oil and gas supplies from the Middle East but also by mitigating the country's reliance on the Straits of Malacca. After extending the crude oil pipelines to Kunming, a refinery and ethylene plant were also built. The pipelines lie underneath the Indian Ocean in the south where the oil and gas would be loaded to the Chinese border in Myanmar's north, where they would help meet China's growing energy needs. These pipelines supported 400,000 barrels of oil a day and 12 billion cubic meters of natural gas a year to China's southern Yunnan province, which had the third lowest GDP per capita of China's administrative divisions. As a major step in Beijing's quest for energy security, it helped Yunnan to diversify its traditional economic structures and supported China's southwestern development. The crude oil is used as the feedstock for a new refinery in Kunming, and Myanmar's natural gas is used for industries in Yunnan Province and beyond. On the other hand, the two pipelines reduced transport costs and time for China. Furthermore, it could establish trade access routes from the Bay of Bengal to Yunnan. According to the developmental strategy, the two pipelines brought new opportunities for China's underdeveloped southwestern provinces. In addition, the refinery and ethylene plant will attract more investments from the Chinese SOEs and big international multinational companies. Therefore, China will gain from its southwest "bridgehead" strategy through connecting with Southeast Asia and South Asia.[42]

Although the pipeline provided the required gas supply to Yunnan Province, in the southwest of China, the villagers of Rakhine in Myanmar who used wood for cooking and candles for light still largely lived in the dark due to insufficient power. Myanmar, the

---

[41] Yearly Approved Amount of Foreign Direct Investment (by country), DICA, Yangon, 2017, p. 4.

[42] Tenzing Chopel Sherpa, Importance of Myanmar in China's Strategic Interest: A Case Study on Sino-Myanmar Oil and Gas Pipelines. Gangtok: Sikkim University, 2016, p. 65.

foreign-recipient state, faced many risks and challenges including insufficient infrastructure, future re-negotiations with China, security concerns, local resistance, and ethnic tensions.[43] In the offshore site, the main impacts affected negatively on fishing, mangrove conservations, etc. Several local interest groups were opposed to the pipelines' (possessive-apostrophe) construction for fear of losing land, jobs, and livelihoods.[44]

While transporting oil in 2017, local fishermen faced difficulties due to the transported-oil ships at the Maday Deep-Sea Port.[45] However, in August 2017, Oil and Petroleum Law in Myanmar recovered the domestic effects, focusing on environmental conservation, the guarantee of energy security in Myanmar, acquisition of tax for the country, and license permission.[46] Therefore, it may protect the life of the local people and prevent negative impacts on domestic politics in Myanmar, the receiving country.

Conclusion

It can be summarized that there are not only pros but also cons for both countries in cooperation. The pros for Myanmar include receiving more FDI, land rental, transit fees, etc. The cons for Myanmar were economic difficulties faced by local people along the pipelines and huge pressure on its environment. The pros for China include the convenient alternative to oil and gas, mitigating the reliance on Straits of Malacca, reducing transport costs and time, and establishing trade access route from Bay of Bengal to Yunnan. The cons for China consist of the high cost of pipelines and increasing resentment of the local

[43] Aye Sapay Phyu, "Myanmar–China Pipeline Construction Under Scrutiny," *Myanmar Times*, January 14, 2013.

[44] "In Search of Social Justice along the Myanmar–China Oil and Gas Pipeline," Myanmar China Pipeline Watch Committee, Mandalay, January 8, 2016, p. 9.

[45] An Interview with U Nay Aung, Manager, Department of offshore oil and gas, MOGE, MOEE, Naypyitaw, Myanmar, October, 2017.

[46] Oil and Petroleum Law in Myanmar, Department of offshore oil and gas, MOGE, MOEE (Naypyitaw: October, 2017).

people of Myanmar along the pipelines toward Chinese business regions.

However, Chinese government has not given up its strategic partnership with Myanmar. Under the new National League for Democratic Government, plans are underway to amend the current laws, bylaws, and regulations to oil and gas exploration in the country. Therefore, it may protect the life of local people and prevent negative impacts on domestic politics in Myanmar, the receiving country.

As Myanmar's oil and gas projects have already been constructed and operated, the best way forward would be for the government of Myanmar and foreign companies to restore the confiscated lands to the farmers who owned them and to prove that they are sharing the benefits of the projects with the affected communities by launching local development programs. In this regard, the priority areas that the project should focus on are, firstly, restoring the damaged farmlands through technical assistance, including provision of mechanized equipment, until the farmers regain the same agricultural yields as they enjoyed before the project started. Moreover, the project should provide livelihood assistance to the affected farmers and launch a conservation plan for forests damaged due to the pipeline construction.

https://doi.org/10.1142/9789811225222_0008

Chapter

8

A Myanmar Perspective on ASEAN–China Environmental Cooperation

Wai Yan Linn

Myanmar Institute of Strategic and International Studies, Myanmar

Introduction

It is irrefutable that the world today is under threat of natural disasters and imminent destruction from the impact of climate change and global warming and the scientific consensus is that the cause or causes is/are in large part anthropogenic. The ASEAN region and its member countries are some of the most vulnerable regions to such natural disasters. There is no need to recount or provide evidence to the audience today about the untold suffering this has caused. The world has witnessed the devastation and the loss in human life and property that have been wrought by cyclones, typhoons storms, tsunamis, and the floods, mudslides and landslides, the earthquakes and volcanic eruptions, the wild forest fires, the air pollution that have shrouded cities, towns, and villages in haze across large parts of southeast Asia and China.

Based on data from Munich Re NatCatSERVICE, think tank Germanwatch issued a report and also ranked countries most affected by weather-based disaster in the last 20 years between 1998 and 2017. In this long-term list, three countries from the ASEAN region, namely Myanmar, the Philippines, and Vietnam, were included, ranking third, fifth, and ninth, respectively. Vietnam experienced 298 reported deaths and $4.05 billion worth of economic losses in 2017. Thailand, ranked 10th on the list, recorded 176 deaths and an estimated $4.37 billion in economic losses. The year 2017 started on a bad note for the country. Myanmar earned its spot on the long-term list due to Cyclone Nargis that slammed into the country in 2008, causing more than 95% of the damage and fatalities in the country over the past decade.[1]

The devastating results of climate change and global warming neither have knowledge nor respect for national boundaries or authority in the form of armed might or riches and wealth nor do they care about who the real perpetrators are. It has become increasingly clear that no one country or race will be held to account — there is no discrimination between the guilty and the innocent.

However, we cannot and should not ignore the need for a better life quality for our people in the region. So there must also be cooperation for socio-economic development in the form of the 17 Sustainable Development Goals, in other words the Global Goals set by the United Nations.

This state of affairs means that the ASEAN 10 + 1 nations must work in cooperation and collaboration not in competition or rivalry, first for the resolution of the environmental crisis the world faces today and secondly to implement sustainable development goals.

This chapter discusses the position of Myanmar and the extent to which it can contribute to a green and healthy environment

[1] Maizura Ismail, "*ASEAN Nations Hard Hit By Natural Disasters*," *The ASEAN Post*, 5 December 2018.

conducive to peace, stability, and prosperity in our Asian region hand in hand with other ASEAN nations and China. Myanmar is a small and still developing nation, in the midst of transition to democracy and facing many challenges, but as a member of ASEAN it has good friends that it can rely on and a good relationship with China that goes back to ancient times. Myanmar is therefore committed toward making worthwhile contributions to the best of its abilities.

About Myanmar

The total land area of Myanmar is 676,578 square kilometers and it shares its boundary of about 6,151 kilometers with India, Bangladesh, China, Laos, and Thailand. The estimated current population is 54.3 million and the population density overall is approximately 80.31 people per square kilometer in 2019. According to the 2014 Census, about 70.4% of the population lives in rural areas and 29.6% in urban areas.[2] Most rural people are farmers, fishermen, or others who earn their livelihood in the agricultural, fishery, and forest sectors.

Myanmar has a tropical climate with three seasons. A cool winter from November to February, a hot summer season from March to April, and a rainy season that starts from May and ends in October.[3]

Myanmar is endowed with rich natural resources including rich biodiversity, forests, abundant water, and mineral resources. Its diverse flora and fauna include more than 11,820 plants, 259 mammals, 1,056 birds, 297 reptiles, 82 amphibians, 775 freshwater and marine fishes, 5 marine turtles, and 52 coral species, making it one of the richest biodiversity centers in Asia and the Pacific.[4]

According to the record of the Myanmar Statistical Information Service (MMSIS), the forest cover of Myanmar in 2017 was

[2] The Republic of the Union of Myanmar, The 2014 Housing and Population Census, May 2015. http://www.dop.gov.mm/en.

[3] Myanmar Climate Change Strategy and Action Plan (MCCSAP) 2016–2030.

[4] *Ibid.*

107,898 square kilometers, which is about 41.3% of total land area of Myanmar.[5]

The economy of Myanmar is based largely on agriculture and employs 70% of labor force in the agricultural sector.[6] The economy is not yet fully industrialized. As a result, the major sources of environmental challenges of Myanmar are not from industrial pollution but from the problem of underdevelopment. The environmental degradation of Myanmar is caused mainly by poverty, the expansion of agricultural land, deforestation, population growth, and pollution of the land and water.

Major Challenges from Air, Land, and Water Pollution of Myanmar

Myanmar has many types of natural resources including natural gas, petroleum, timber, minerals and gemstones, and hydropower potential. In early 1990s, the government of Myanmar introduced market reforms and allowed private sector enterprises and foreign investments. Sudden influx of interested private investors and foreign enterprises encroached upon Myanmar's rich natural resources. For example, Myanmar lost a total of 1.7 million hectares of forest cover from 2001 to 2013. Forest depletion before 2009 stood at 97,000 hectares a year. Since then it has risen to an average of 185,000 hectares a year. Myanmar's deforestation rates are among some of the highest in the entire region. Satellite data show the region where much of the logging has taken place. In terms of percentage, Myanmar lost 5.7% of its tree cover, from 2001 through 2014.[7]

In fact, legal logging is not the major cause for deforestation. The principal factors for the huge loss of forest would be illegal forest

---

[5] Central Statistical Organization, "Forest Cover Status in Myanmar", January 13, 2020, http://mmsis.gov.mm/statHtml/statHtml.do?orgId=195&tblId=DT_YAF_0003&conn_path=I2.

[6] FAO in Myanmar, Myanmar at a glance http://www.fao.org/myanmar/fao-in-myanmar/myanmar/en/.

[7] *Myanmar: Agriculture, Natural Resources, and Environment Initial Sector Assessment, Strategy, and Road Map*. Mandaluyong City, Philippines: Asian Development Bank, 2013.

exploitation. Moreover, some of the forest areas are depleted by illegal agricultural expansion and firewood extraction. According to the report of the 2014 Housing and Population Census, 69.2% of households use firewood as their main source of energy. Deforestation is the major environmental problem in Myanmar. So is the pollution of water resources such as lakes, creeks, and rivers especially with used plastic bags and unmanageable waste and garbage.

Another challenge from the environmental problems in Myanmar rests on the growing population and its need for economic development. Overpopulation affects forests because they destroy a lot of trees for resettlement, agriculture, and household fuel. About 70.4% of the population lives in rural areas and most of the rural people rely on forests for their basic needs and income. This is one of the factors for deforestation.

Unsustainable agricultural practices, such as the overuse of chemical fertilizers and pesticides, are of great environmental concern. For example the total mass of pesticides applied by farmers increased by 331% between 2009 and 2010, and many of these will ultimately end up polluting water resources.[8]

Another cause for the environmental problems in Myanmar is urban expansion and internal migration. Urbanization and internal migration have recently been gaining attention in Myanmar. Attention to migration is due to the consequences of climate change and natural hazards. For instance, many people have been forced to migrate and find new sources of income as a result of changing rainfall patterns and pest infestations. Similarly, Cyclone Nargis which hit the Ayeyarwady Delta in May 2008 indirectly forced many to migrate to Yangon. Under the conditions of rapid urbanization in Myanmar, large-scale conversion of farmland into building land is unavoidable. This trend adversely shapes the environment on a large scale. As settlements expand, urbanization leads to: losses of bio-productive land; decline of biodiversity; reduction of permeable surface areas required

[8]David A. Raitzer, Jindra Nuella G. Samson and Kee-Yung Nam, Achieving Environmental Sustainability in Myanmar, *ADB Economics Working Paper Series*, No. 467, December 2015.

for recharging groundwater; and shrinkage of open space required for fresh air production. It also creates problems of sewage and garbage disposal, which have adverse impact on health.

Nevertheless, the growing population, increased urbanization and industrialization will exert increasing pressure on the natural resources of the country. While some of the resources such as forests, flora and fauna, fisheries, and marine resources are renewable, mineral resources like petroleum, coal, and gems are effectively non-renewable. Therefore, Myanmar's environmental considerations have to be properly integrated with development planning, keeping in mind the need for environmentally sound and sustainable utilization of our natural resources.

Myanmar's Experience in Policy Formation and Implementation

To coordinate environmental matters in the country, the Government of the Union of Myanmar formed the National Commission for Environmental Affairs (NCEA) in February 1990 with the Minister for Foreign Affairs as its Chairman. The Commission was later affiliated to the Ministry of Forest since the work of environmental protection and conservation was considered to be more akin to this Ministry. The aims of the establishment of the NCEA were: (i) to advise the government on environmental policies; (ii) to act as a coordinating body for environmental affairs; and (iii) to promote environmentally sound sustainable development.

Environmental Policy (1994)

Building on the 1994 National Environmental Policy of Myanmar, this Policy reiterates the following core values:

- The wealth of the nation is its people, its cultural heritage, its environment, and its natural resources.
- It is the responsibility of the State and every citizen to preserve its natural resources in the interests of present and future generations.

- Environmental protection should always be the primary objective in seeking development.

Myanmar Agenda 21 (1997)

The NCEA in 1997 issued the Myanmar Agenda 21 for the new millennium.

- To mobilize and focus national efforts to achieve sustainable development.
- Policies, strategies, and actions to be taken in the social, economic, and environmental dimensions are clearly defined in the Agenda.

National Sustainable Development Strategy (NSDS) (2009)

The NSDS is also an important step and guiding document to fully implement in harmony and balance among the three main pillars of environment, economic, and social sectors. It has identified the short, medium, and long-term goals for sustainable development. NSDS therefore is more comprehensive in incorporating environmental consideration into social and economic development than Agenda 21 to ensure the achievement of Sustainable Development.

Myanmar's NSDS vision is "Wellbeing and Happiness for Myanmar People". Three goals identified are as follows:

Goal 1: Sustainable Management of Natural Resources;
Goal 2: Integrated Economic Development;
Goal 3: Sustainable Social Development.

Sustainable management of natural resources in Myanmar, from the environmental perspective, comprises 11 areas, namely:

(1) Sustainable forest resources management;
(2) Biodiversity conservation;
(3) Sustainable freshwater resources management;
(4) Environmental quality management and enhancement;

(5) Sustainable management of land resources;
(6) Sustainable management of coastal, marine and island ecosystems;
(7) Sustainable management of ecotourism;
(8) Sustainable management of mineral resources utilization;
(9) Sustainable management of agriculture, livestock and fisheries;
(10) Sustainable energy production and consumption;
(11) Sustainable industrial, transport and communication development.

Environmental Conservation Law (2012)

Environmental Conservation Law was enacted in 2012 with the following objectives:

(1) To implement the Myanmar National Environmental Policy;
(2) To lay down the basic principles and give guidance for systematic integration of the matters of environmental conservation in the sustainable development process;
(3) For the emergence of a healthy and clean environment and to conserve the natural and cultural heritage for the benefit of present and future generations;
(4) To reclaim ecosystems that are starting to degenerate and disappear;
(5) To manage and mitigate the decrease and loss of natural resources through sustainable use;
(6) To promote public awareness and cooperation;
(7) To promote international, regional and bilateral cooperation in the matters of environmental conservation;
(8) To cooperate with Government departments, Government organizations, international organizations, non-government organizations, and individuals in matters of environmental conservation.

There are also Environmental Conservation Rules (2014), Environmental Impact Assessment Procedures (29 December, 2015) and Environmental Quality Emission Guidelines (29 December 2015).

It must, however, be noted that no country can in this day and age fulfill these goals, plans, and projects all on its own. As stated at the beginning of the chapter, it must work in cooperation with nations and organizations with common goals.

Cooperation between ASEAN and China in Environmental Conservation

ASEAN cooperation on climate change

That the ASEAN countries are highly vulnerable to climate change is because a large portion of their populations live and earn their livelihood in coastal areas. Moreover, the main livelihood of the people is in the agriculture sector and they are therefore dependent on land, water, and forestry resources. So the current climate crisis is a major concern to ASEAN.

A study carried out by Asian Development Bank projects a 4.8°C rise in mean annual temperature and a 70 centimeters rise in mean sea level by 2100 in Indonesia, the Philippines, Thailand, and Vietnam. A rise in sea level would result in major problems for many of ASEAN's largest coastal cities, such as Jakarta, Bangkok, and Manila.[9] It is going to have an impact on millions of people who may be uprooted from their original homes with loss of property and income. There will be greater increase of greenhouse gas emissions in the atmosphere due to loss of forests to absorb the gases and this in turn will have adverse effects on human health.

ASEAN member states (AMS), though not the source of significant emission of greenhouse gases, have taken actions to address climate change through various environmental, economic, and social activities over the years. Indonesia has announced that it will reduce emissions by 26%, Malaysia by 40% in terms of energy intensity of GDP by 2020 compared to 2005 level and Singapore to a level of

[9] ASEAN Cooperation on Climate Change https://environment.asean.org/asean-working-group-on-climate-change/.

16% and below.[10] Many AMS have also begun to include adaptation measures in development planning.

Collectively, ASEAN countries have been responding to climate change by focusing on the implementation of relevant actions in the ASEAN Socio-Cultural Community (ASCC) Blueprint 2009–2015.

This was clearly stated at the 40th Meeting of the ASEAN Multi-Sectoral Framework for Climate Change: Agriculture and Forestry Towards Foods and Nutrition Security and Achievement of SDGs held at Ha Noi, Vietnam on 11 October 2018 that

> The ASEAN Socio-Cultural Community (ASCC) Pillar supervises all ASEAN programs for cooperation and joint activities on climate change through the ASEAN Climate Change Initiative (ACCI) that works under the purview of the ASEAN Senior Officials on Environment (ASOEN). The ASEAN Working Group on Climate Change (AGWCC) is the implementing arm of the ACCI through the ASEAN Joint Response to Climate Change.[11]

ASEAN–China Cooperation for Climate Change

In May 2016, China and ASEAN jointly adopted the ASEAN–China Strategy of Environmental Cooperation (2016–2020) which set cooperation on environmental data and information sharing as one of the cooperation priorities.

The ASEAN–China Strategy of Environmental Cooperation (2016–2020) aims to strengthen the relationship between China and Southeast Asia countries regarding environmental protection and regional sustainable development.

The overall objective of the ASEAN–China strategy on environmental cooperation is to take a coordinated and integrated approach to address environmental issues by taking into consideration national circumstances as well as the obligations under multilateral environmental agreements. The specific objectives include:

---

[10] *Ibid.*
[11] *Ibid.*

(1) Enhancing high-level policy dialogue with a focus on environmental issues of common concern to increase understanding, enhance cooperation and secure the harmonization of interests of ASEAN and China;
(2) Enhancing dialogue and cooperation on environmental protection;
(3) Improving capacity for national and regional environmental management through sharing knowledge and experiences and implementing joint actions;
(4) Enhancing cooperation on priority areas, improving effectiveness and quality of cooperation, and developing good practices for regional and South and South environmental cooperation;
(5) Supporting ASEAN Community's Post-2015 Vision.

The areas of cooperation include:

(1) Environmental data and information sharing;
(2) Risk assessment and management;
(3) Biodiversity and ecological conservation;
(4) Environmental industry and technology for green development;
(5) Environmental sustainable cities;
(6) Education and public awareness;
(7) Institutional and human capability building;
(8) Joint research.

In 2017, the ASEAN–China Environmental Cooperation Plan (2016–2020) was adopted, which decided to develop an implementation plan and established the ASEAN–China Environmental Information Sharing Platform (EISP). The objectives of EISP are as follows:

(1) Promote the interconnectivity and interoperability of environmental information between China and ASEAN;
(2) Improve the ability to collect, sort, analyze, process, and use environmental information and data;

(3) Narrow the gap in development, improve environmental management and standardization;
(4) Further improve South–South environmental cooperation and promote regional green and sustainable development.

At this point, the author would like to bring attention to how the ASEAN + China partnership can enhance sustainable development for the ASEAN Region, on the one hand, and also promote environmental protection of the region as a whole, on the other. In doing so, the author would like to refer to China's Belt and Road Initiative (BRI) and the Second Belt and Road Forum that was hosted by China in Beijing from April 25–27. Around 37 heads of state, 360 government ministers, and 100 leaders of international organizations were among the 5,000 participants that gathered in Beijing for the second Belt and Road Forum, to discuss their signature infrastructure project, which began in 2013 to rebuild ancient trading routes across Eurasia. It is first and foremost an initiative to bring together people across the world with bridges, railways, and highways as well as opening the old maritime Silk Road — to enhance people-to-people connectivity, which is talked about so much but with little being done to make it a reality. There are of course nations that are opposed to this opening up of the world, thinking it is being done with ulterior motives. But many Asian nations including the ASEAN nations believe that this BRI will not only help alleviate poverty and hunger but will also contribute greatly to the mitigation of climate change and global warming and all its ills. Here, the author would like to share the UN Secretary General's thoughts on the BRI, which he stated clearly would facilitate the 2030 Agenda Sustainable Development Goals in his speech at the BRI Forum. The 2030 Agenda is our globally-agreed plan for people, peace, planet, and prosperity, but financial resources are inadequate for the developing countries to reach those goals by 2030. Secondly, he said that "climate change is running faster than we are. I have repeatedly called it the defining issue of our time. Climate change poses an existential risk to all countries." Moreover, he remarked that land and ocean temperatures, sea levels, and greenhouse gas concentrations this year are the highest recorded in the last four years. Natural disasters are wrecking the environment and threatening people's health. The poor and the weak suffer the most. But what the Secretary General also stated is there is hope because although there are extreme challenges, there are also promising trends. China's leadership on climate action is helping to show the way.[12] He recounted how:

> New renewable energy jobs in China now outnumber those created in the oil and gas industries. In 2017, China invested over $125 billion dollars in renewable energy, an increase of at least 25 per cent over the previous year. And China's new cutting-edge transmission line that sends electricity along a pathway 600 miles longer than anything built to date is a further potential boon for renewables.[13]

And as stated earlier, people-to-people connectivity will help to forge closer bonds and understanding and with understanding will come tolerance for different manners, customs, and beliefs. This will also help to eliminate racial, cultural, religious, and all kinds of intolerance and misunderstanding. It will contribute toward one of the cooperation areas of ASEAN–China Strategy of Environmental Cooperation, that is, the institutional and human capability building.

Myanmar's Contribution

Myanmar, as an ASEAN member nation that China knows very well, is still making honest and determined endeavors from being classified as a "Least Developed Country" to fulfill the people's goal for full democracy. Industrially, we have yet to catch up with other members of the ASEAN and have to depend on international aid and assistance for further development. We are endowed with rich natural resources, but most of these resources are also exhaustible and non-renewable. But we wish to be a responsible member in the regional and

[12] United Nations Secretary-General, "Secretary-General's remarks at the opening ceremony of the Belt and Road Forum for International Cooperation", 26 April 2019, https://www.un.org/sg/en/content/sg/statement/2019-04-26/secretary-generals-remarks-the-opening-ceremony-of-the-belt-and-road-forum-for-international-cooperation.

[13] *Ibid.*

world community, so any contribution we make must be realistic and sustainable. We therefore cannot contribute much in the way of high-tech innovations. But we have one very vibrant and inexhaustible resource in our youths. Our youths are dedicated, idealistic, and courageous and are a credit to our nation. In any campaign for the development or humanitarian endeavor, they are ready to sacrifice their time and energy for any good cause. In Myanmar, even under authoritarian rule, they were active and enthusiastic regarding the campaign against illiteracy and won the Shah Pahlavi Prize in the year 1971. Today, they are active in the fight against Plastic Pollution. This is not only the case of youths in urban areas but also rural areas. They have joined movements to establish "Trash Free Villages" and "Plastic and Garbage Free Wards" in towns and villages. They have formed small non-governmental organizations to provide schooling to destitute street children to get recruited for activities sponsored by such movements as the ASEAN–China Green Envoys Program (GEP). The GEP, which attaches great importance to the special role of the public awareness and participation by youths and has made a lot of effort in this area, will surely welcome the participation of Myanmar youths. More opportunities to attend the meetings, seminars, and training courses like the Youth Seminar on Green Development held in May 2012 in Beijing, the Youth Seminar on Green Economy and Ecological innovation in September 2012 in Beijing and, the Youth Seminar on Green School in July 2013 in Beijing would be of great benefit. GEP is also active in ASEAN+3 Youth Environment Forum hosted by ASEAN. Participants from both China and ASEAN member countries have been involved in GEP. Moreover, GEP boosts the construction of the cooperation network among regional youth for more public participation and higher awareness.

This would benefit not only our youths but also other young people in the region. There would be mutual exchanges of ideals and ideas that would benefit not only these young people but future generations as well. So ASEAN+1 should look to the future and invest in our youth.

https://doi.org/10.1142/9789811225222_0009

Chapter

9

A View on ASEAN and China Cooperation Strategy in Environmental Protection

Daw Htay Htay Nyein

Myanmar Institute of Strategic and International Studies (MISIS), Myanmar

Introduction

How is environment defined nowadays?

Environment can be defined as everything that creates our surroundings and influences our ability to live on the Earth — the air that we breathe, the water that covers most of the Earth's surface, the plants and animals around us, and much more. Since several decades, scientists have been carefully observing people's actions that have an effect upon the environment. It was found that human beings are causing air pollution, deforestation, acid rain, and other problems that are harmful both to the Earth and to themselves. Nowadays, "the environment" often refers to the overall condition of our planet, or how healthy it is.[1]

Relations between ASEAN and China

The Association of Southeast Asian Nations (ASEAN) states and China are neighboring countries and share common boundaries of mountains and rivers, similar history, cultures, and traditions. China's contact with the ASEAN began at the 24th ASEAN Ministerial Meeting in July 1991 in Kuala Lumpur, where Malaysia and China were granted the status of ASEAN Consultative Dialogue Partners. Subsequently ASEAN set the path for China's admission into the ASEAN Regional Forum in 1994 and eventually China became a full dialogue partner at the 29th ASEAN Ministerial Meeting (AMM) in July 1996 in Jakarta, Indonesia.[2]

Since its inception in 1997, the China–ASEAN cooperation mechanism has played an important role in promoting China–ASEAN cooperation, having reinforced the process of regional political and economic cooperation and promoting mutual understanding and common ground on cooperation between China and ASEAN.[3] The ASEAN Committees of Beijing (ACB) were also established by the ASEAN Heads of Missions in Beijing to promote ASEAN–China relations. In December 1997, then President Jiang Zemin and ASEAN leaders organized their first ever summit and issued a joint statement in which they announced their decision to establish a 21st century-oriented partnership of good neighborhood and mutual trust between China and ASEAN.[4] Due to China's dynamic economic growth, its relations with ASEAN states have grown significantly. In the wake of economic and social development in China and ASEAN,

---

[1] *Fact Monster*, "What is the Environment?" 2019. https://www.factmonster.com/math-science/earth-environment/what-is-the-environment.

[2] "Overview of ASEAN–China Dialogue Relations." https://googleweblight.com.

[3] "ASEAN China Strategy of Environmental Cooperation (2009–2015)." www.chinaaseanev.org>about>functions.

[4] Zou Keyuan, "China–ASEAN Relations and International Law," 2009. https://books.google.co.id/books/about/China_Asean_Relations_and_International.html?id=JQWkAgAAQBAJ&redir_esc=y (October 3, 2019).

China–ASEAN cooperation has been widened to the fields of the environment, science and technology, non-traditional security areas, and related legal issues.[5] Environmental protection has become a priority area in the ASEAN–China cooperation. Protecting the environment, reducing environmental pollution, and curbing ecological deterioration through the strengthened cooperation led to contribute to the common interests of China and ASEAN member states (AMS).[6]

Contextual Background

Background

Environmental degradation becomes a great challenge to the economic and social development in the world. The international community broadly recognizes sustainable development as a development strategy. Therefore, to promote environmental cooperation at national, regional, and international levels it is essential for countries to implement sustainable development goals.

While addressing environmental problems, most developing countries often find obstacles in the field of sustainable development, such as inequitable development both within and among countries, environmental pollution and ecological degradation, lack of funds and technologies, and insufficient institutional and human capacity. Moreover, the international financial crisis, climate change, food and energy shortage, and intensive natural disasters make the burden heavier for the developing countries to realize sustainable development.[7]

---

[5] John Wong, Keyuan Zou and Huaqun Zeng, "China–ASEAN Relations: Economic and Legal Dimensions." https://books.google.co.id/books?id=TMrICgAAQBAJ&printsec=frontcover&dq=China%E2%80%93ASEAN+Relations:+Economic+and+Legal+Dimensions.&hl=zh-CN&sa=X&ved=2ahUKEwiPrtP1iObsAhUZA4gKHcMdCYoQ6AEwAHoECAAQAg#v=onepage&q=China%E2%80%93ASEAN%20Relations%3A%20Economic%20and%20Legal%20Dimensions.&f=false.

[6] "ASEAN China Strategy of Environmental Cooperation (2016–2020)." https://www.greengrowthknowledge.org/national-documents/asean-china-strategy-environmental-cooperation-2016–2020.

[7] "Environment and Development Challenges — Conservation." https://www.conservation.org/docs/default-source/publication-pdfs/ci_rioplus20_blue-planetprize_environment-and-development-challenges.pdf.

Over the past decades, Asia-Pacific region, as the biggest and the most diversified region in the world, encountered rapid economic growth and partial achievement of the Millennium Development Goals. Nevertheless, the region still has a huge poor population. By depending upon goods and services provided by sound environment and ecosystem, they are surviving. That is the reason why achieving sustainable development is especially critical for this region.[8]

If ASEAN–China environmental cooperation is strengthened, this will benefit the developing countries in this region. This will have a good impact on the environmental quality and conservation of the natural ecosystem. This will consequently lead to the improvement of economic development quality, people's welfare, and the achievement of long-term developments goals.[9]

The ASEAN side

When the UN Conference in Stockholm in 1972 agreed on the Stockholm Declaration, it drew the attention of ASEAN to examine the common environmental problems on a regional as well as national level. Recognizing the significance of environmental cooperation for sustainable development and regional integration, ASEAN has closely cooperated to promote environmental cooperation among its member states since 1977.[10] The United Nations Environment Programme (UNEP) was instrumental in encouraging ASEAN to adopt its first regional policies on the environment and has, indeed, remained an important influence in supporting the cooperative environmental initiatives in Southeast Asia. In 1977, UNEP commissioned an ASEAN Sub-regional Environment Programme (ASEP). Environmental awareness and environmental regionalism have evolved

---

[8] "Asia-Pacific Sustainable Development Goals Outlook — Asian." Asian Development Bank https://www.adb.org/sites/default/files/publication/232871/asia-pacific-sdgoutlook-2017.pdf.

[9] "ASEAN–China Strategy on Environmental Cooperation >asean › environment › wp-content › uploads › 2017/02 › ASEAN-China-S." https://books.google.com.mm › books.

[10] Wakana Takahashi, *Environmental Cooperation in Southeast Asia*. https://iges.or.jp/en/pub/environmental-cooperation-southest-asia.

slowly in three major phases. The first phase of ASEAN-sponsored environmental cooperation covers the period from 1978 to 1982.

In the first phase, ASEAN introduced the first sub-regional environment program (ASEAN Environmental Programme (ASEP I)) which mainly emphasized on securing the availability of natural resources for economic development. The ASEAN environment ministers adopted two further such programs, the second (ASEP-II) for the years 1983 to 1987 and the third (ASEP-III) for the four years from 1988 to 1992. During the second phase, the focus shifted to transnational threats. The third phase is characterized by the formation of formal relations within the community.[11] ASEAN started its ASEAN Strategic Plan of Action on the Environment 1994–1998. This was followed by the Hanoi Plan of Action 1999–2004, which was formulated pursuant to ASEAN Vision 2020 and covered some 15 areas relating to the environment. Besides, the Vientiane Action program 2004–2010 sought to realize an "ASEAN Socio-Cultural Community" and to promote "Environmental Sustainability".[12]

The ASEAN Community has been building efforts, and has experienced significant progress in the environment sector.[5] Progress has been made in the following 11 priority areas of cooperation as outlined in ASEAN Socio-Cultural Community Blueprint 2009–2015:

(1) Addressing global environmental issues;
(2) Managing and preventing transboundary environmental pollution;
(3) Promoting sustainable development through environmental education and public participation;

---

[11] Koh Kheng Lian, Nicholas A. Robinson and Heng Lye Lin, *ASEAN Environmental Legal Integration: Sustainable Goals?* Cambridge: Cambridge University Press, 2016. https://books.google.co.id/books?id=aEnGCwAAQBAJ&printsec=frontcover&dq=ASEAN+Environmental+Legal+Integration:+Sustainable+Goals?&hl=zh-CN&sa=X&ved=2ahUKEwiGyM6gkubsAhWZxYsBHY0BDUMQ6AEwAHoECAMQAg#v=onepage&q=ASEAN%20Environmental%20Legal%20Integration%3A%20Sustainable%20Goals%3F&f=false.

[12] Daniel C. Esty and Maria H. Ivanova, *Global Environmental Governance: Options & Opportunities.* Forestry & Environmental Studies Publications, Series 8, 2002. https://elischolar.library.yale.edu/fes-pubs/8.

(4) Promoting Environmentally Sound Technology (EST);
(5) Promoting quality living standards in ASEAN cities/urban areas;
(6) Harmonizing environmental policies and databases;
(7) Promoting the sustainable use of coastal and marine environments;
(8) Promoting Sustainable Management of Natural Resources and Biodiversity;
(9) Promoting the sustainability of freshwater resources;
(10) Responding to Climate Change and addressing its impacts;
(11) Promoting Forest Sustainable Management.

There are five key programs. These are implementation of ASEAN Peatland Management Strategy including the 5-year International Fund for Agricultural Development — Global Environment Facility (IFAD-GEF) project on rehabilitation of Peatland forests in Southeast Asia, implementation of ASEAN Environmental Education Action Plan, development of ASEAN Guidelines on Eco-schools, and implementation of ASEAN Heritage Parks Program and ASEAN Environmentally Sustainable City Award Program.[13]

China's side

With the aim to establish a beautiful country, the Chinese government decided to comprehensively deepen the reforms, by making systemic and institutional reforms for environmental protection, promoting ecological civilization in 2013. Acceleration of the establishment of the ecological civilization system, improvement of the administration of territorial management, resources conservation, and environmental protection were initiated.[14]

China has conducted the most strenuous efforts and undertaken the most substantial measures in ecological and environmental

[13] "ASEAN–China Strategy on Environmental Cooperation asean › environment › wp-content › uploads › 2017/02 › ASEAN–China-S."
[14] *Ibid.*

protection with the fastest progress for several years and best outcomes achieved. To tackle the domestic environmental challenges, China has signed over 30 multilateral conventions and protocols related to the environment. In 2016 alone, the Ministry of Environmental Protection had hosted 12 environmental training courses for the developing countries, with participation of around 280 environment officials and experts from 43 countries, including 80 from ASEAN countries. Representatives of ASEAN countries appreciated China's achievements in environmental protection and praised China for its great efforts and support for promoting ASEAN's environmental cooperation.[15]

Action Plans and Progress

Considerable progress has been made since the establishment of China–ASEAN strategic partnership between China and ASEAN. The environmental cooperation between China and ASEAN provides regional social and economic cooperation. It also promotes the mutual understanding and friendship among China and ASEAN. Environmental protection is being prioritized in ASEAN–China cooperation.[16]

Primary goal

The primary goal between ASEAN and China is to build a resource-conserving, environmentally friendly society. Through strengthened cooperation, protecting the environment, reducing environmental pollution, and reducing ecological deterioration are the common interests. In 2003, China and ASEAN signed Joint Declaration of the Heads of State/Government of the Association of Southeast Asian

---

[15]"China, ASEAN to Further Deepen Environmental Cooperation: Official." http://www.xinhuanet.com//english/2017-09/14/c_136607357.htm.

[16]"ASEAN-China Strategy on Environmental Cooperation (2016–2020)", January 2016, https://www.greengrowthknowledge.org/national-documents/asean-china-strategy-environmental-cooperation-2016-2020.

Nations and the People's Republic of China on Strategic Partnership for Peace and Prosperity. This declaration emphasizes that we should strengthen cooperation through "more exchanges in science and technology, environment, education, culture, personnel", and should enhance "mutual cooperation mechanisms in these fields".[17]

Cooperation activities

Both China and AMS are developing countries faced with similar problems such as environmental pollution, depletion of natural resources, loss of biodiversity, ecosystem degradation together with rapid growth of economy, growth of population, and acceleration of industrialization and urbanization. To deal with these challenges, China and AMS have adopted a series of effective policies in combination with various measures, and made remarkable progress in promoting green and sustainable development.[18] Within the framework of cooperation strategy and its action plan, ASEAN and China have performed lots of cooperation activities. These include cooperation on high-level policy dialogues, ASEAN–China Green Envoys Program (GEP), biodiversity and ecological conservation, environmental industry and technology, and joint research, etc. These relate to the enhancement of South–South environmental cooperation.[19]

Adoption of ASEAN–China Strategy on Environmental Protection Cooperation (2009–2015)

At the 11th China–ASEAN Summit in November 2007, environmental protection was listed as the 11th priority area for cooperation under the mechanism of China–ASEAN Summit, and the Chinese Premier Wen Jiabao stated that China was prepared to establish a

---

[17] *Ibid.*

[18] *Ibid.*

[19] *Ibid.*

China–ASEAN environmental cooperation center, proposing to jointly develop an ASEAN–China strategy on environmental cooperation and improve related cooperation. In 2009, "ASEAN–China Strategy on Environment Protection Cooperation (2009–2015)" was adopted by the Ministry of Environmental Protection of China and Environment Division of the ASEAN secretariat.[6] The overall objective is to make efforts in ASEAN–China cooperation on agreed priority areas of environmental protection by taking a coordinated and step-by-step approach with a view to achieve environmental sustainability in the region. This cooperation has six priority areas as follows:

(1) Public awareness and environmental education;
(2) Environmentally sound technology, environmental labeling and cleaner production;
(3) Biodiversity conservation;
(4) Environmental management capacity building;
(5) Cooperation on environmental goods and services;
(6) Global environmental issues.

Adoption of ASEAN–China Environmental Cooperation Action Plan (2011–2013)

In 2011, the "ASEAN–China Environmental Cooperation Action Plan (2011–2013)" was developed and adopted by China and ASEAN. The actions are to perform high-level policy dialogue on environmental cooperation, to start and implement the ASEAN–China GEP, to cooperate on biodiversity and ecological conservation, to promote the exchange between environmental industry and technology, and to do joint research. The China–ASEAN Environmental Cooperation Center and the Environment Division of the ASEAN secretariat were appointed for coordination and implementation.[20]

[20] "China–ASEAN Strategy on Environmental Protection Cooperation." www.cn-asean.org › uploadfile.

Adoption of ASEAN–China Environmental Cooperation Action Plan (2014–2015)

After the completion of the ASEAN–China Environmental Cooperation Action Plan (2011–2013) in 2013, China and ASEAN held the "Seminar on ASEAN–China Environmental Cooperation: Review and Prospect" in April 2013. In that seminar, they reached consensus to formulate a new action plan. Negotiation was reached on the content of the new action plan during the seminar. China and ASEAN jointly formulated and adopted "ASEAN–China Environmental Cooperation Action Plan (2014–2015)" in 2013. Themes to strengthen policy dialogue on environmental cooperation by organizing ASEAN–China Environmental Cooperation Forum; to carry on implementation of the ASEAN–China GEP; to increase cooperation on biodiversity and ecological conservation, environmental industries and technology; and to develop ASEAN–China Environmental Outlook were discussed.

Establishment of the China–ASEAN Environmental Cooperation Center

Under the approval of the Chinese Government, the Ministry of Environmental Protection set up the China–ASEAN Environmental Cooperation Center in March 2010[21] to promote environmental cooperation among China and ASEAN. The center has set the following goals:

(a) To serve as a Focal Point for environmental cooperation between China and ASEAN;
(b) To provide support to the government agencies both in China and in AMS for developing cooperation strategy/plan on environment;
(c) To play the key role and provide technical support on coordination and implementation of the programs and projects;

[21] *Ibid.*

(d) To facilitate the dialogues on environment and development policy, including the proposed China–ASEAN environment ministerial level meeting and other high level environmental exchange activities;
(e) To promote the cooperation on environmental technology in the business community and the exchanges between public and private sectors;
(f) To conduct joint policy study on selected key issues in the region, and provide the policy recommendations to policy makers;
(g) To develop partnership with all interested countries and international organizations and build up a network to support the programs and activities jointly developed by China and ASEAN.

Organizing ASEAN–China Environmental Cooperation Forum

ASEAN–China Environmental Cooperation Forum is an essential platform for China and ASEAN to conduct high-level policy dialogue, share information and experiences, promote pragmatic cooperation and exchanges in the area of environment. The forum emphasized on ASEAN–China environmental issues of common concern, with the participation of policymakers, entrepreneurs, academicians, and experts from China, ASEAN, international organizations, non-governmental organizations, etc.[22]

The first ASEAN–China Environmental Cooperation Forum was held in Nanning, China, in October 2011. The theme of the Forum was "Innovation and Green Development". The second ASEAN–China Environmental Cooperation Forum was held in Beijing, China, in September 2012. The theme of the Forum was "Biodiversity and Regional Green Development". The third ASEAN–China Environmental Cooperation Forum was held in Guilin, Guangxi province, in September 2013. The theme of the Forum was "Building

[22] "China–ASEAN Environmental Forum Commences in Beijing." *China Daily › cn › China › Environment.*

up Partnership for Regional Green Transformation". The fourth ASEAN–China Environmental Cooperation Forum was held in Nanning, Guangxi province, in September 2014. The Forum was themed "National Strategy and Regional Cooperation for Sustainable Development: New Challenges and New Opportunities".[23] The China–ASEAN Environmental Cooperation Forum: Policy Dialogue and Workshop on Environmentally Sustainable Development was held in Nanning, China, in September 2015 organized by the China–ASEAN Environmental Cooperation Centre (CAEC).[24]

On September 11, 2018, China–ASEAN Environmental Cooperation Forum was held in Nanning with the topic of "Big Data Driven Innovation in Ecological Environmental Protection".[25] Since 2011, ASEAN–China Environmental Cooperation Forum has been held regularly. ASEAN–China Environmental Cooperation Forum plays a significant role in strengthening environmental cooperation between ASEAN and China and promoting sustainable development in the region.

Launching and Implementing ASEAN–China GEP

The ASEAN–China GEP was officially initiated in October 2011. The program includes Green Innovation (capability building for government decision makers), Green Pioneer (awareness and education for youth) and Green Entrepreneur (establishment of partnership among enterprises for green development).[26] To perform the cooperation

---

[23] *Ibid.*

[24] "China–ASEAN Environmental Cooperation Forum: Policy Dialogue and Workshop on Environmentally Sustainable Development." https://environment.asean.org/china-asean-environmental-cooperation-forum-policy-dialogue-and-workshop-on-environmentally-sustainable-development-16-18-september-2015-nanning-china/.

[25] "China–ASEAN Environmental Cooperation Center." https://www.devex.com/organizations/china-asean-environmental-cooperation-center-64708.

[26] "ASEAN-China Strategy on Environmental Cooperation (2016–2020)", January 2016, https://www.greengrowthknowledge.org/national-documents/asean-china-strategy-environmental-cooperation-2016-2020.

strategy, under the framework of ASEAN–China GEP, ASEAN and China implemented following activities:

(1) Capacity building for policy makers. GEP has suggested capacity-building projects to decision makers from ASEAN via forums and workshops to meet the demands for green development and regional cooperation. Several projects have been conducted for this purpose.[5]
(2) Environmental education and public awareness for youth. GEP has shown great importance to the special role of the public awareness and participation by youth and has made a lot of efforts in this area, such as the Youth Seminar on Green Development in May 2012 in Beijing. ASEAN member countries have been involved in GEP.
(3) Besides support from institutions like Asian Development Bank, Center for Environmental Education and Communications of Ministry of Environmental Protection of China, etc., GEP has established a good relationship with environmental administrations both from China and ASEAN since its launch, as well as ASEAN Secretariat and other relevant institutes.[27]

Promoting cooperation on biodiversity and ecological conservation

Biodiversity conservation is one of the priorities identified by the Strategy 2009–2015. The aim is to support China and ASEAN to increase capacity to develop and implement policies, plans, and actions on biodiversity and ecological conservation. ASEAN and China carried out personnel exchanges, held the ASEAN–China seminar on biodiversity conservation cooperation, and developed "Case studies on China–ASEAN biodiversity and ecological conservation" which was published in 2013.

With the support of the UNEP and in collaboration with ASEAN Center for Biodiversity, the China–ASEAN Environmental

[27] *Ibid.*

Cooperation Center organized the "Workshop on ASEAN–China implementation of biodiversity conservation strategy and Aichi target capacity building" and "Seminar on China–ASEAN biodiversity conservation practice" in Kunming, China, in July 2013.[28]

With the support of UNEP, the China–ASEAN Environmental Cooperation Center and ASEAN Centre for Biodiversity together with international experts are developing the "ASEAN–China policy instruments and cooperation practices on biodiversity conservation" which was completed in 2014.[29]

Advancing cooperation on environmentally sound technology and industry

Environmentally sound technology and industry is a critical area in the "ASEAN–China Environmental Protection Cooperation Strategy". While deepening regional economic integration and the emphasis on environmental problems, environmental technology and industry cooperation is hoped to play an important role in the future.

In 2012, CAEC developed the "ASEAN–China Cooperation Framework for Environmentally Sound Technology and Industry" with the support of the Ministry of Environmental Protection of China and the ASEAN Secretariat. This aims to support a platform for China and the ASEAN to strengthen cooperation in environmentally sound technology and industry. The actions outlined in the framework include setting up a network for environmentally sound technology and industrial cooperation, establishing a service platform, establishing demonstration base, and developing pilot projects, etc.[30]

In October 2013, Premier Li Keqiang proposed to establish a China–ASEAN Demonstration Base for Environmental Technology and Industry cooperation as an initiative for China–ASEAN environmental industry cooperation at the 16th China–ASEAN Summit. In May 2014, the Ministry of Environmental Protection in Yixing,

---

[28] *Ibid.*

[29] *Ibid.*

[30] *Ibid.*

China, supported by ASEAN Secretariat and ASEAN, held the Conference on China–ASEAN Environmental Industry Cooperation. The ASEAN–China Cooperation Framework for Environmentally Sound Technology and Industry was initiated and the China–ASEAN Demonstration Base for Environmental Technology and Industry Cooperation (Yixing) was inaugurated at the conference.[31]

Conduct joint policy research

China and ASEAN are working together to prepare the China–ASEAN Environment Outlook as required in the Action Plan. The ASEAN–China Environment Outlook is framed to analyze and assess the status and future development trend of cooperation on environment and development between China and ASEAN from a regional perspective, to provide necessary knowledge, experience and tools for deepening environmental cooperation and further promoting regional sustainable development. The ASEAN–China Environment Outlook themed "Towards Green Development" emphasizes the evaluation of green development status in China and ASEAN, analyzes major problems facing China and ASEAN in respect to environment and development, and summarizes the main policies and measures and best practices for promoting green development by China and ASEAN, as well as provides policy recommendations on green development.[32]

The application submitted by China–ASEAN Environmental Cooperation Center for support from China–ASEAN Cooperation Fund was approved. In February 2014, the kick-off meeting for China–ASEAN Environment Outlook project was held in Beijing, attended by ASEAN Secretariat representatives, members of core panels (including ASEAN, Chinese and international experts), and eight representatives from relevant international institutions. This meeting agreed on the outline and framework of the report, and defined the overall orientation of Outlook, division of tasks, and timeline.

---

[31] *Ibid.*

[32] *Ibid.*

This ASEAN–China Environment Outlook was due to be completed in 2015.[33]

Objectives and Principles of Cooperation

Objectives of cooperation

The overall objective of the ASEAN–China Strategy on Environmental Cooperation (2016–2020) is to strengthen ASEAN–China cooperation in priority areas of environmental protection by taking a coordinated and integrated approach with a view to achieving environmental sustainability in the region.[34] The specific objectives of the ASEAN–China Strategy on Environmental Cooperation (2016–2020) are as follows:

(a) Enhancing high-level policy dialogue with focus on environmental issues of common concern to increase understanding, enhance cooperation, and secure the harmonization of interests of ASEAN and China;
(b) Enhancing dialogue and cooperation on environmental protection;
(c) Improving capacity for national and regional environmental management through sharing knowledge and experiences and implementing joint actions;
(d) Enhancing cooperation on priority areas, improving effectiveness and quality of cooperation, and developing good practices for regional and South–South[1] environmental cooperation; and
(e) Supporting ASEAN Community's Post-2015 Vision.[35]

Principles

The principles for guiding ASEAN–China environmental cooperation are as follows:

---

[33] *Ibid.*
[34] China–ASEAN Environment Outlook 1 (CAEO-1): Towards Green Development. https://books.google.com.mm › books.
[35] *Ibid.*

(a) taking coordinated and integrated steps to address global and regional environmental issues by taking into account obligations under multilateral environmental agreements (MEAs) [to which countries are parties to], as well as national circumstances and development status;
(b) Conducting cooperation and dialogue on an equal position within the mandate and responsibilities of environmental authorities; and cooperation is based on the principles of mutual benefits, consultation and consensus.[36]

Areas of Cooperation

Policy dialogue and exchange

Objective: To provide various platforms for China and ASEAN environmental policymakers (GC) to exchange views on major regional environmental issues, to share environmental management experience, to improve cooperation by taking joint actions, and to carry out the consensus reached by China and ASEAN leaders.
Activities:

(a) Organizing ASEAN–China Environmental Cooperation Forum;
(b) Organizing ASEAN–China Environment Ministers Meeting at an appropriate time.[37]

Environmental data and information management

Objective: To enhance ASEAN and China's capacity to collect, process and utilize environmental data and information activities:

(a) Developing ASEAN–China joint platform on environmental information sharing, a cooperation initiative made at the 17th ASEAN–China Summit;

---

[36] *Ibid.*
[37] *Ibid.*

(b) Conducting knowledge and experience sharing on environmental information and data by taking into account the possibility of harmonization of environmental standards;
(c) Conducting capacity-building activities on collection, processing, and use of environmental information and data.[38]

Environmental Impact Assessment (EIA)

Objective: To enhance ASEAN and China's capacity in the field of environmental impact assessment through knowledge and experience sharing activities:

(a) Conducting capacity building cooperation on EIA;
(b) Conducting joint research on environmental impact assessment and management.[39]

Biodiversity and ecological conservation

Objective: To further develop and implement the ASEAN–China Cooperation Plan on Biodiversity and Ecological Conservation in collaboration with ASEAN Centre for Biodiversity, so as to improve China and AMS's capacity and consciousness in developing policies, strategies or action plans with regard to biodiversity conservation, implementing the Convention on Biological Diversity and other international obligations, promoting the conservation, management, and sustainable use of biological resources.[40]

Activities:

(a) Sharing experience on ecological protection in both urban and rural areas and carrying out cooperation on demonstration projects;

---

[38] *Ibid.*
[39] *Ibid.*
[40] *Ibid.*

(b) Enhancing capacity for biodiversity protection to contribute to poverty alleviation, and climate change mitigation and adaptation;
(c) Promoting cooperation on priority biodiversity conservation areas such as ASEAN Heritage Parks;
(d) Promoting cooperation on marine environmental protection areas such as mangrove reserve, coastal zone planning, coral reefs restoration, and marine liter pollution control;
(e) Exploring the potential of biodiversity and strengthening the monitoring of the current ecological conservation and demonstration cooperation;
(f) Promoting collaboration on scientific research in areas such as land-based pollution management, climate change research;
(g) Conducting study on policy tools, practices of biodiversity and ecological conservation. Such studies would include but not be limited to:
  (i) The economy of ecosystem services and biodiversity;
  (ii) Fair and equitable sharing of the benefits from the utilization of genetic resources and associated traditional knowledge;
  (iii) Management and eradication of invasive alien species;
  (iv) Private sector engagement;
  (v) Raising awareness for biodiversity conservation and sustainable use of its components;
(h) Enhancing capacity to implement the Strategic Plan for Biodiversity 2011–2020 and its Aichi Biodiversity Targets.[41]

Promoting environmental industry and technology for green development

Objective: To implement the ASEAN–China Cooperation Framework for Environmentally Sound Technology and Industry by building up a platform for information exchange, conducting demonstration projects and developing joint research on environmental technology, in

[41] *Ibid.*

support of the 10-Year Framework on Sustainable Consumption and Production.

Activities:

(a) Implementing ASEAN–China Cooperation Framework for Environmentally Sound Technology and Industry;
(b) Strengthening communication and cooperation among government agencies, entrepreneurs, research institutes, researchers and 11 associations in environmental protection industry between China and AMS by organizing conference on China–ASEAN environmental industry cooperation regularly and creating a platform for sharing experiences and promoting technology transfer among enterprises in China and ASEAN;
(c) Conducting collaborative research on environmental technology pollution prevention and treatment, and carrying out related training projects;
(d) Continuing to promote demonstration bases and explore appropriate equipment and cooperation methods for AMS by selecting specific cooperation projects and trying to conduct bilateral technological cooperation between China and specific AMS;
(e) Enhancing knowledge sharing in environmental labeling products certification, organic certification, good agriculture practice attestation, and other mechanisms such as green supply chain to promote sustainable consumption and production;
(f) Promoting bilateral cooperation on environmental labeling to establish China–ASEAN Environmental Labeling Alliance for green trade development.[42]

Environmentally sustainable cities

Objective: Improving the capability in promoting environmentally sustainable cities in China and ASEAN including small and growing

[42] *Ibid.*

urban areas through knowledge and experience sharing as well as network and partnership building.

Activities:

(a) Conducting knowledge and experience sharing on urban ecological conservation to promote ecologically friendly urban development;
(b) Strengthening cooperation on sustainable production and consumption in the context of urbanization;
(c) Conducting cooperation on environmentally sound treatment and disposal of urban waste with linkage to the ASEAN Clean Air, Clean Water, Clean Land Initiative;
(d) Promoting cooperation to strengthen climate change mitigation and adaptation in environment-friendly and climate resilient cities where supplementary activities are conducted under the ASEAN Action Plan on Joint Response to Climate Change (AAP-JRCC) under the ASEAN Working Group on Climate Change (AWGCC);
(e) Developing Environmentally Sustainable Cities (ESC), model cities through public and multi-partner participation;
(f) Promoting cooperation with linkage to ASEAN ESC Model Cities program;
(g) Promoting the use of certificates and awards as incentive measures;
(h) Promoting a network to share knowledge and experiences on urban forestry/forest management.[43]

Environmental education and public awareness

Objective: Enhancing ASEAN–China public awareness on environmental protection through exchanges and cooperation between environmental education institutions as well as relevant government

---

[43] *Ibid.*

agencies and civil society of China and AMS, and supporting the implementation of the ASEAN Environmental Education Action Plan (AEEAP) 2014–2018.

Activities:

(a) Continuously implementing GEP for more actions in personnel exchange, capacity building, and policy dialogues;
(b) Setting up a platform for knowledge, know-how, and good practices sharing for more public participation, through linkage with ASEAN Environmental Education Inventory Database;
(c) Supporting eco-schools in AMS and developing the cooperation network among youth in China and AMS, encouraging discussions on emerging environmental issues and promoting linkage with other international youth networks within the region for more knowledge sharing for joint efforts;
(d) Mobilizing resources among China and AMS for enhancing the implementation of environmental education and public awareness nationwide.[44]

Institutional and human capability building

Objective: To enhance capacity of environmental management in China and AMS through various means under GEP.

Activities:

(a) Strengthening comprehensive training for environment management personnel and enhancing capacity for policy formulation on environmental economics and environment and health;
(b) Providing a platform for sharing experience on enforcement of environmental laws, and relevant legislations;

[44] *Ibid.*

(c) Conducting mutual visits and personnel exchanges of environment management personnel to improve their capacity for environment management in China and AMS.[8]

Joint research

Objectives: To promote communication and exchange and capacity building among scholars and think tanks in order to forge green think tanks in China and ASEAN.

Activities:

(a) Developing and releasing the China–ASEAN Environment Outlook;
(b) Carrying out studies on global and regional emerging environmental and development issues of common concern in China and ASEAN, and sharing the outcome of the studies through existing ASEAN–China cooperation mechanism in order to provide targeted, scientific and information-based policy recommendations for policymakers.[45]

Implementation Arrangements

Institutional arrangement

The Ministry of Environmental Protection of China and the environmental authorities of ASEAN will provide guidance and support for implementation of the strategy. The environmental authorities of China and AMS will keep each other informed of their respective focal points for the implementation of the strategy.[46]

The China–ASEAN Environmental Cooperation Center and the Environment Division of ASEAN Secretariat shall take charge of

[45] *Ibid.*

[46] "ASEAN-China Strategy on Environmental Cooperation (2016–2020)", January 2016, https://www.greengrowthknowledge.org/national-documents/asean-china-strategy-environmental-cooperation-2016-2020.

coordination and communication for the implementation of the strategy. The China–ASEAN Environmental Cooperation Center shall serve as the main implementation agency of the strategy, in collaboration with its ASEAN counterpart institutions to develop plans of actions and milestones to implement the activities identified in the strategy.[47]

Funding mechanism

The funding source and other supporting source for the implementation of the strategy include but are not limited within the following:

(a) ASEAN–China cooperation fund;
(b) Other funds provided by the government of China;
(c) Support in cash or in kind provided by China and AMS on voluntary basis;
(d) Funds donated by international partners or third countries;
(e) Funds donated by private sector.

The fund will be used to support the implementation of the strategy or other cooperation activities agreed by the two sides.[48]

Forms of cooperation

Cooperation can be conducted in accordance with ASEAN and China's laws, rules, [AMS] regulations, national policies [AMS], and practices as well as the needs and funding availabilities. The emphasis of the cooperation particularly the capability-building activities should be placed on the lesser developed countries in accordance with Initiative for ASEAN Integration.[49] The cooperation will take various forms by taking a long-term and programmatic approach. AMS and

---

[47] *Ibid.*
[48] *Ibid.*
[49] *Ibid.*

China will encourage wider and deeper participation of local organizations into ASEAN–China environmental cooperation.

Conclusion

As far as we have observed, cooperation strategy between China and ASEAN has been well-established. Forums were held periodically. Strategies were adopted and projects were carried out in a timely manner. There are a variety of fields that cover environmental protection such as policy dialogue and exchange, environmental data and information management, environmental impact assessment, biodiversity and ecological conservation, and promoting environmental industry and technology for green development. Each project has its own principles and objectives. If the two institutions cooperate together with the same pace and implement regular plans, then the burden of environmental harm will decrease more and more. Cooperation from international level to regional level and from regional level to district level will be of great help to protect environmental conditions around ASEAN and China.

https://doi.org/10.1142/9789811225222_0010

Chapter 10

Singapore's Sustainable & Clean Energy Development: A Case Study

Tai Wei Lim

East Asian Institute, National University of Singapore, Singapore

Introduction

Singapore's vision for a sustainable and clean energy development is enveloped in its goal of becoming a "livable city". Singapore envisions the concept of "livability" in the following manner. First, it wants to be a competitive economy in order to attract investments and provide jobs.[1] Right from the start of its nation-building days, Singapore has adopted a pragmatic worldview, which is not to impede economic development by making environmental urban planning part and

[1]Centre for Liveable Cities, *Singapore and Civil Service College, Liveable and Sustainable Cities a Framework*. Singapore: Centre for Liveable Cities, Singapore and Civil Service College, Singapore, 2014, p. 6.

parcel of development. Indeed, this pragmatic approach was made known to the rest of the world. Minister for the Environment and Water Resources Masagos Zulkifli delivered Singapore's national statement at the United Nations High-Level Political Forum (HLPF) on Sustainable Development in New York City on 18 July 2018, where he emphasized pragmatism trumps ideological goals when it comes to instituting policies for the environment and resource use through people-centered policies.[2]

Basic Worldview

The pragmatic worldview when it comes to development is also reflected in its awareness that Singapore has no choice but to be a sustainable environment because "the city has to survive with limited natural resources, especially in terms of land and water."[3] In this sense, it matches the overall pragmatic approach that Singapore espouses when building up a livable city or when formulating policies for the environment and resources. This has been the case since nation-building. Minister for the Environment and Water Resources Masagos Zulkifli reiterated:

> Singapore has always put its people at the centre of all its development policies … Our economic transformation is a story about uplifting our people's lives, by providing good education, health, housing, employment and a clean environment … We take a pragmatic approach to policymaking and governance, focusing on outcomes, not ideology, to foster a harmonious, inclusive and prosperous society.[4]

---

[2] *Channelnewsasia*, "Singapore Takes Pragmatic Approach to Sustainable Development: Masagos," 18 July 2019, accessed July 18, 2019. https://www.channelnewsasia.com/news/singapore/masagos-united-nations-sustainable-development-10540344.

[3] Centre for Liveable Cities, *Singapore and Civil Service College, Liveable and Sustainable Cities a Framework*. Singapore: Centre for Liveable Cities, Singapore and Civil Service College, Singapore, 2014, p. 6.

[4] *Channelnewsasia*, "Singapore Takes Pragmatic Approach to Sustainable Development: Masagos," 18 July 2019, accessed July 18, 2019. https://www.channelnewsasia.com/news/singapore/masagos-united-nations-sustainable-development-10540344.

Along with the spirit of pragmatism, there is a growing realization that Singapore is a tiny island vulnerable to climate change and global warming as it is located at a low sea level and is a highly urbanized territory. Thus, in 2016, Singapore ratified the Paris Agreement to manage climate change and global warming alongside 120 states to commit to cutting down emissions intensity by 36% below 2005 levels by 2030.[5] Therefore, Singapore was a full participant in the 2018 Year of Climate Action with nearly 250,000 Singaporeans, firms and non-profit organizations (NPOs) coming together to affirm they are making efforts to mitigate climate change and shrink their carbon footprint, an approach known as "collaborative multi-stakeholder partnerships" as the state alone is limited in means.[6]

More for Less

With rapid economic development and as Singapore reaches a high standard of living, the government and its citizens expect a "high quality of life, including the social and psychological well-being of the population."[7] These developmental goals for a livable city are not to be taken for granted as natural order of things because, historically, modernization theories had situated economic developmental goals ahead of well-being, apart from urban planning, and with hindsight, consideration for sustainability. Thus, Singapore's goals are counter-intuitive when it comes to developmental priorities. Singapore is one of the few states in the world that manages to achieve a high standard

---

[5] Han Wei Jason Tan, "Hydrogen a More Sustainable Bet for S'pore's Energy Future," September 28, 2019, *Today Online.* https://www.todayonline.com/commentary/hydrogen-more-sustainable-bet-spores-energy-future.

[6] *Channelnewsasia*, "Singapore Takes Pragmatic Approach to Sustainable Development: Masagos," July 18, 2019, accessed July 18, 2019. https://www.channelnewsasia.com/news/singapore/masagos-united-nations-sustainable-development-10540344.

[7] Centre for Liveable Cities, *Singapore and Civil Service College, Liveable and Sustainable Cities a Framework.* Singapore: Centre for Liveable Cities, Singapore and Civil Service College, Singapore, 2014, p. 6.

of living and economic well-being without overly polluting its environment. For one, it has moved into alternative energy use.

Solar Power

To meet the objectives of energy efficiency and reliability, the Singapore government ventured into solar and other alternative fuels. The government has implemented this objective in some of its large-scale projects. For example, the Singapore state inserted solar panels in all new Housing & Development Board (HDB or Singapore's well-known and reputable public housing system) projects, and the expenditure of installation has been reduced by 40% in 2017 compared to previous years.[8] Another victory scored was when the HDB instituted the fourth solar leasing tender under the SolarNova program, gathering the collective efforts of multiple agencies in solar panels use across 1,218 HDB blocks and 49 government sites.[9]

The shift from the more polluting fossil fuels puts Singapore on course to be a lower carbon footprint country embracing the cleaner solar power as an alternative energy source. Singapore absorbs an average yearly solar irradiance of 1,580 kW per meter square per hour, and up to 50% more solar radiation than that of other northern/southern hemisphere states in the temperate belt of world regions.[10] Current technologies capture solar power by using photovoltaic cells. With growth expected in this energy sector for Singapore, there are already above 1,500 solar panels installed in the island state, powering

[8] Han Wei Jason Tan, "Hydrogen a More Sustainable Bet for S'pore's Energy Future," September 28, 2019, *Today Online*. https://www.todayonline.com/commentary/hydrogen-more-sustainable-bet-spores-energy-future.

[9] Housing and Development Board (HDB), "HDB-EDB Joint Press Release — HDB Exceeds 2020 Solar Capacity Target with Fourth SolarNova Tender Launch," December 14, 2018, accessed December 14, 2018. https://www.hdb.gov.sg/cs/infoweb/about-us/news-and-publications/press-releases/hdbedb-joint-press-release-hdb-exceeds-2020-solar-capacity.

[10] Han Wei Jason Tan, "Hydrogen a More Sustainable Bet for S'pore's Energy Future," September 28, 2019, *Today Online*. https://www.todayonline.com/commentary/hydrogen-more-sustainable-bet-spores-energy-future.

130 MW peak of electricity (2% of Singapore's total electricity demand).[11] The idea or strategy therefore is not to replace conventional fuels but to turn to alternative energy fuels as a backup reserve fuel. In the fourth SolarNova tender, HDB has sunk plans for building a total solar capacity of 230 megawatt-peak (MWp) for more than 4,550 HDB buildings, outpacing the agency's own target of 220 MWp by 2020 and it is also on target to install solar power in 5,500 HDB blocks by 2020.[12]

The main challenges for Singapore's solar power industry are the cloudy conditions of tropical Singapore, large number of towering skyscrapers that block sunlight from reaching the panels and the lack of space for the panels. Because of these challenges, experts project solar power can only meet 5% of the total electricity demand by the year 2020, so some proposed solutions to resolve such challenges are to keep conventional power generators in reserve to keep electricity supply going when solar power conditions are impeded or less than ideal.[13] Besides technical challenges, there are also challenges in costs of solar power when compared with cheaper fossil fuel-based power generation. A non-technological solution in lowering costs of solar power is simply cost-sharing. HDB is the biggest player in solar panel facilities in Singapore and a designated central procurement agency for solar panels, but it has farmed out the installation procedures and costs to multiple stakeholders with each successful tender with other government organizations taking charge of solar panels constructions in their own buildings through power purchase agreements.[14]

[11] *Ibid.*

[12] Housing and Development Board (HDB), "HDB-EDB Joint Press Release — HDB Exceeds 2020 Solar Capacity Target with Fourth SolarNova Tender Launch," December 14, 2018, accessed December 14, 2018. https://www.hdb.gov.sg/cs/infoweb/about-us/news-and-publications/press-releases/hdbedb-joint-press-release-hdb-exceeds-2020-solar-capacity.

[13] Han Wei Jason Tan, "Hydrogen a More Sustainable Bet for S'pore's Energy Future," September 28, 2019, *Today Online*. https://www.todayonline.com/commentary/hydrogen-more-sustainable-bet-spores-energy-future.

[14] Housing and Development Board (HDB), "HDB-EDB Joint Press Release — HDB Exceeds 2020 Solar Capacity Target with Fourth SolarNova Tender Launch,"

Hydrogen as Energy

Besides solar power, another source examined since at least 2017 is hydrogen gas as the government carried out trials in the coastal areas of Semakau Island, with the hope of harnessing hydrogen which has the largest energy content of any common fuel by weight, and can itself behave like an energy carrier to transport, keep and disseminate energy.[15] Semakau itself is iconic of sustainable resource management. Semakau Landfill is situated approximately 8 km south of the main Singapore Island, where a 7 km peripheral rock bund bordered by impermeable membrane and marine clay envelops part of the maritime sea areas off Pulau Semakau and Pulau Sakeng to construct the landfill space.[16] Thus, space is created from this landfill for test bedding the storage and production of hydrogen gas, cells, and manufacturing facilities.

Because hydrogen can keep energy for later use, they are effective in batteries. Solar power can produce electrical power that energizes electrolysis for hydrogen storage and when converted to hydrogen fuel cells, they can then produce electricity on demand.[17] Therefore, besides conventional power generators, hydrogen fuels can also be a backup option when solar power is impeded by natural conditions. Most importantly, the whole process is pollution-free and can be used for a variety of purposes. Like all other alternative energy sources, hydrogen has its own limitations. The issue of cost comes into play as electrolysis powered by solar power is 2–3 times more expensive than

---

December 14, 2018, accessed December 14, 2018. https://www.hdb.gov.sg/cs/infoweb/about-us/news-and-publications/press-releases/hdbedb-joint-press-release-hdb-exceeds-2020-solar-capacity.

[15] Han Wei Jason Tan, "Hydrogen a More Sustainable Bet for S'pore's Energy Future," September 28, 2019, *Today Online*. https://www.todayonline.com/commentary/hydrogen-more-sustainable-bet-spores-energy-future.

[16] National Environment Agency (NEA), "Semakau Landfill," April 27, 2018, accessed April 27, 2018. https://www.nea.gov.sg/our-services/waste-management/3r-programmes-and-resources/waste-management-infrastructure/semakau-landfill.

[17] Han Wei Jason Tan, "Hydrogen a More Sustainable Bet for S'pore's Energy Future," September 28, 2019, *Today Online*. https://www.todayonline.com/commentary/hydrogen-more-sustainable-bet-spores-energy-future.

when the process uses carbon-based fuels like natural gas.[18] Thus, there is literally a price to pay when using a much cleaner fuel. In the solar power case, the government agencies involved managed to pare down the prices of solar power. They adopted a business model of solar leasing, where a centralized agency like HDB farms out the upfront cost for solar panel installation by going into a power purchase agreement with a private sector developer paying for solar power consumption at a preferential rate equivalent or lower than the prevailing electricity tariff rate.[19] Perhaps such models can be of reference for the hydrogen fuel industry.

Besides costs, space is also needed to build big-sized holding areas for hydrogen mass production and these spaces necessitate the use of strong, heavy compression-protected holding containers for storing hydrogen. Hydrogen itself is explosive, so such safe and secure equipment and facilities are extremely crucial.[20] Hydrogen is a colorless and odorless gas so any leakage from the holding tanks are difficult to detect and yet they can cause spectacular explosions. History is filled with manmade disasters involving hydrogen explosions. Counter arguments however insist that contemporary high-tech equipment are so safe that they stand less chance of explosions compared to gasoline and other flammable gases.

The hydrogen cells also need high temperatures to work well, requiring a platinum catalysis to attain such high temperatures. Such catalysts are expensive. Cheaper catalysts or alternatives to create high temperature conditions have yet to materialize. Therein lies the urgency to solve this problem in order to utilize literally limitless potential of hydrogen. However, if Singapore is truly committed to

---

[18] *Ibid.*

[19] Housing and Development Board (HDB), "HDB-EDB Joint Press Release — HDB Exceeds 2020 Solar Capacity Target with Fourth SolarNova Tender Launch," December 14, 2018, accessed December 14, 2018. https://www.hdb.gov.sg/cs/infoweb/about-us/news-and-publications/press-releases/hdbedb-joint-press-release-hdb-exceeds-2020-solar-capacity.

[20] Han Wei Jason Tan, "Hydrogen a More Sustainable Bet for S'pore's Energy Future," September 28, 2019, *Today Online*. https://www.todayonline.com/commentary/hydrogen-more-sustainable-bet-spores-energy-future.

developing and exploiting solar energy resources, then some opine that the scale of solar power use can offset the costs of using solar power for generating high levels of power for carrying out photo-electrolysis.[21] In fact, Singapore had been looking at Fuel Cell and Hydrogen technologies since at least 2001 and Singapore built up capabilities in research and development (R&D) that caught the attention of fuel cell firms that are coming up with potential applications where fuel cell and hydrogen technologies can be used to reduce emission levels and improve the energy efficiency.[22]

Some want the government to take a lead in this by making hydrogen fuel cell usage a policy goal, particularly in providing backup generation of power, building facilities with compression tanks for hydrogen production, and/or for the transport authority to approve use of hydrogen fuel cells in vehicles.[23] Other uses include: grid storage and power distribution, grid balancing, transportation, emission control for generators, combined cooling, heat and power for buildings, back-up power for data centers, disaster relief application, and onsite generation for remote sites such as islands.[24] Besides private sector companies, research institutions like the Energy Storage group at ERI@N are also looking into such cutting-edge applications. The Energy Storage group at ERI@N [Energy Research Institute at Nanyang Technological University (NTU)] has a staff strength of about 30 researchers/students/staff situated in the Research Techno Plaza, Department of Material Science and Engineering, and the Clean Tech One (armed with a new Prototyping Lab) to test the

[21] *Ibid.*

[22] Energy Research Institute at Nanyang Technological University (NTU) [ERIAN}, "Energy Storage and Fuel Cell," October 25, 2016, accessed October 25, 2016. http://erian.ntu.edu.sg/Programmes/IRP/ESFC/Pages/Home.aspx.

[23] Han Wei Jason Tan, "Hydrogen a More Sustainable Bet for S'pore's Energy Future," September 28, 2019, *Today Online*. https://www.todayonline.com/commentary/hydrogen-more-sustainable-bet-spores-energy-future.

[24] Energy Research Institute at Nanyang Technological University (NTU) [ERIAN}, "Energy Storage and Fuel Cell," October 25, 2016, accessed October 25, 2016. http://erian.ntu.edu.sg/Programmes/IRP/ESFC/Pages/Home.aspx.

viability of scaling-up of such technologies and/or applications.[25] All these facilities are located near or with NTU campus for easy access and collaborative teamwork.

Concluding Remarks and the Near Future

A third alternative option is biomass gasification. It has the clear advantage of turning Singapore's wastes into fuels. Another advantage is the presence of a home-grown solution through scientific innovation. Scientists have found a method of manufacturing hydrogen by using a widely available *E. Coli* Bacteria to convert wastes to energy. This solution is still in trial stages but carries promises of a sustainable and clean energy use in the future. Hopefully, the *E. Coli* Bacteria solution can follow the footsteps of solar power where a centralized government agency has taken the lead to coordinate the cost-sharing of solar panel installation and solar power generation. This multiple-stakeholders approach can be a potential model for the *E. Coli* Bacteria energy production solution. It can also learn from the hydrogen gas trials where the users eliminated two birds with one stone, as the saying goes. The use of a landfill for energy storage and production is a progressive strategy. The public is also put at ease as there are membranes to prevent leachate from the refuse leaking out from the landfill and ancillary facilities were constructed to facilitate the landfill operations becoming self-sustainable.[26]

---

[25] *Ibid.*

[26] National Environment Agency (NEA), "Semakau Landfill," April 27, 2018, accessed April 27, 2018. https://www.nea.gov.sg/our-services/waste-management/waste-management-infrastructure/semakau-landfill.

https://doi.org/10.1142/9789811225222_0011

Chapter

11

Challenges for Municipal Solid Waste Management in Vietnam

Nguyen Thi Phuong Lan

Thuy loi University (TLU), Ha noi, Vietnam

Introduction

Nowadays, there are more and more people moving from rural areas into large cities with a dream of making more money to support their families and improve their living standards. Therefore, urbanization has now become one of the most important issues and challenges for Vietnam in efforts to pursue sustainable development.

Vietnam's population in 2018 was approximately 96 million. According to World Population Review, population density of Vietnam in 2018 was 291.33 persons per kilometer square. This makes Vietnam the 15th most densely inhabited country. It is obvious that urbanization at a quick pace and without any proper planning will lead to many issues such as insufficient accommodation, education, health care, public services, transportation, and waste management.[1] Without proper planning system of waste management, people are more likely to be exposed to diseases and other health risks. Recently, many cases of environmental violations have been discovered in the country; the results of those cases are very serious, and it takes a long time for the environment to recover. They also impacted negatively on the economy and health of many people. There were cases where many villages in Vietnam were called cancer villages because the locals there had to use polluted water as their only water supply over a long time.

The increase in waste generation due to rising population and waste generation rate becomes a challenge for Vietnam government to establish proper municipal solid waste (MSW) management. In recent years, MSW management in Vietnam has been paying serious attention to different levels of governments as well as the community. Weak waste management is a common growing problem faced by developing countries. Specific action at the international level needs to be established, so as to inspire and encourage new forms of cooperation, partnership, coordination at all levels, in order to contribute effectively to the provision and improvement of waste management services.

Generation and Characterization of MSW

According to Vietnamese Environmental Protection Law issued by National Assembly in June, 2014, the term Waste is defined as "matters discharged from production, business, services, daily life activities or other activities."

The Decree No. 38/2015/ND-CP on Waste and Scraps Management defines Solid Waste (SW) as "waste in solid or semi-solid (also called sludge) discharged from the production, business, services, daily life activities or other activities."

[1] N. Truong, *Solid Waste Management in Vietnam: Current Situation, Challenges and Strategies for Development*. Helsinki: Metropolia University of Applied Sciences, 2018.

Table 1 Classification of solid waste in Vietnam

Way of Classification	Component
By source of generation	Domestic solid waste
	Industrial solid waste
	Medical solid waste
	Agricultural solid waste
	Construction solid waste
	Sludge
By toxicity	Ordinary solid waste
	Hazardous solid waste

Solid waste classification or sorting can be carried out in many ways. Based on their origin, solid wastes can be classified as urban MSW, construction solid waste, rural solid waste, agricultural solid waste, and medical solid waste. On the other hand, based on their toxic level, solid wastes can be classified as: hazardous solid waste and normal solid waste. Depending on each way of sorting there are differences in the volume and components of solid wastes (see Table 1).

Solid waste in Vietnam can be grouped broadly into three categories:

- Municipal Waste — comprises residential, commercial, and market wastes;
- Industrial Waste — includes hazardous waste from the processing activities of factories and other manufacturing units; clinical wastes from hospitals and clinics; sewage and sludge from municipal sewer systems; construction and demolition waste;
- Agricultural Waste — comprises animal (pigs, cows, and buffaloes) manure from the farmers' houses, crop residues (mainly from coffee, rubber, tobacco and coconut), and residues of agrochemicals.

Identifying Challenges in MSW Management in Vietnam

Rapid increase in waste volume and types

In recent years, the pace of population growth and urbanization has always been associated with the process of industrialization. Vietnam is a developing country with the third highest population density in Southeast Asia and 14th in the world with rapid urbanization, industrialization, population growth, a growing middle-income class, and changing consumption patterns.

The amount of solid waste generated in Vietnam has been increasing steadily over the last decade. For urban domestic solid waste, the amount generated depends on the size of the urban population. Not only has the composition of waste changed but the amount of waste generated also differs. Urban residents make up only one-quarter of the population, yet produce half of the solid waste.

While in 2014, the volume of urban domestic solid waste generated was about 32,000 tons/day. Particularly in Hanoi and HCMC (Ho Chi Minh City), the domestic solid waste generated was 6,420 tons/day and 6,739 tons/day, respectively. According to the calculation, the increase in the waste from 2011 to 2015 averages 12% per year and is on the trend, the level of urban solid waste generation will continue to increase in the near future.[2] The generated waste volume will then increase in the future and is estimated to reach a total of around 69 million tons in 2020 and 91 million tons by 2025.[3] Many open dumping sites and landfills, especially those in large cities, are always overloaded as the total volume of solid waste is increasing remarkably every year but the land is a limited resource. However, there has not been much progress in waste reduction in Vietnam. There is no effort in trying to reduce domestic waste generation (Table 2).

The composition of MSW is also different between urban and rural areas. The hospital and industrial wastes are predicted to increase

---

[2] MONRE. *National Environment Report for Period 2016.* 2016, p. 88.

[3] N. Truong, *Solid Waste Management in Vietnam: Current Situation, Challenges and Strategies for Development.* Helsinki: Metropolia University of Applied Sciences, 2018.

Table 2 MSW generation per capita in 2007–2010

Year	MSW Per Capita (kg/person/day)	References
2007	0.75	MONRE National Environment Report 2011
2008	0.85	—
2009	0.95	—
2010	1.00	—
2015	1.2	Estimated/projected by the VEA in the MONRE National Environment Report 2011
2020	1.4	—
2025	1.6	—

Source: N. T. Thang, *Country Chapter*. 2017.

considerably in the key economic zones and in Mekong Delta. The hazardous wastes such as dry and wet batteries, electric waste, household chemical solvents, and non-degradable waste (plastic, metal, and glass) are increasing in urban waste due to the fast development of industrialization and urbanization. There is a high percentage of organic matter (54–87%) in the waste and also a diversified waste fraction (organic matter, paper, metal, glass, textile, plastic and rubber, ceramic and brick, hazardous, and miscellaneous) (Table 3).

Treatment technology is still limited

In Vietnam, three main waste treatment methods are landfill, microbiological fertilizer production, and burning. Only 30% of the existing landfills meet green standards, while most of the nearly 300 incinerators nationwide are small scale. There are only about 30 facilities producing organic fertilizers from waste at present.

- **Landfilling:** Treatment technology is still limited in Vietnam as landfilling is still the main method of waste treatment. The waste treatment and disposal alternatives in Vietnam have implicit environmental and human risks by the poorly operated landfills and open dumps.

Table 3. Urban solid wastes generated between 2007 and 2010

Content	2007	2008	2009	2010
Urban population (million people)	23.8	27.7	25.5	26.22
% of the urban population in the total population	28.20	28.99	29.74	30.2
Urban solid waste generation indicator (kg/person/day)	~0.75	~0.85	0.95	1.0
Total volume of urban SW generated (tone/day)	**17,682**	**20,849**	**24,225**	**26,224**

Source: N. Truong, *Solid Waste Management in Vietnam: Current Situation, Challenges and Strategies for Development*. Helsinki: Metropolia University of Applied Science, 2018.

As in other countries in Southeast and South Asia, open and controlled dumps are the dominant forms of waste disposal in Vietnam and cause environmental degradation. Landfilling is the common disposal method for MSW in Vietnam as well as for some industrial waste and health care waste. Up to 2015, there were 660 centralized landfills in operation in Vietnam, but only 203 were sanitary landfills (mostly in major cities). In the remaining landfills, most of the solid wastes are buried without care. These disposal sites lack a leachate collection system, protection at the bottom by a geo-membrane or clay-lined layer — a collection equipment, giving rise to serious environmental degradation.[4]

Thus, this practice of waste treatment causes serious health problems for the locals living around the dump sites. However, the overloading status has occurred at many open dumping sites and landfills.

Although there are many environmental pollution problems associated with the disposal of MSW at open dumping and landfill sites, it appears that landfill would continue to be the most widely adopted practice in Vietnam in the coming years, during which certain improvements will have to be made to ensure a sanitary environment.

---

[4] MONRE. *National Environment Report 2018: Solid Waste*. 2018.

Open burning and incineration: Open burning at landfill sites is a common practice in a few cities with the purpose of lowering the total volume of waste at those sites as well as increasing the capacity of the sites. Open burning can also be observed as the main practice for managing domestic solid waste in some countryside areas and in most of the rural areas. Local people in those poor areas burn their solid waste right in their home yards. However, these practices of open burning introduce a large amount of pollutants straight into the atmosphere. In the area of health, a majority of hospitals burn health waste in manual incinerators without exhaust treatment systems. Some hospitals have installed modern incinerators, but they are not under operation due to ambient residential areas.

As a consequence of this practice, humans are at a higher risk of being exposed to and suffering from serious health problems.

Composting: Composting represents the decomposition of organic wastes under controlled conditions to produce compost product that can be further used as soil conditioner or fertilizers. With a high organic matter content, the MSW in Mekong Delta's provinces has a great potential for composting (Byer *et al.,* 2006).[5] However, waste composting is not widely used in the region for a number of reasons including inadequate requirements of biological processes such as poor feed stock or nutrient requirements, poor quality of output fertilizers, and even reduced potential market. Besides, the bio-products from old landfills that were biodegraded by natural processes can be utilized as fertilizers. Presently, more private companies carry out composting for the city's MSW with similar composting technologies at a small scale. Another reason for making composting less attractive is the farmers' habit of using inorganic fertilizers instead of compost.

---

[5] Byer, Philip H., Chi Phuong Hoang, Thi Thuc Thuy Nguyen, Sangeeta Chopra, Virginia Maclaren, and Murray Haight. "Household, Hotel and Market Waste Audits for Composing in Vietnam and Laos." *Waste Management & Research* 24, No. 5 (October 2006): 465–472. https://doi.org/10.1177/0734242X06068067.

At-source segregation and recycling: According to Environmental Protection Law, the waste generators are responsible for sorting waste at source in order to facilitate its re-use, recycling, energy recovery, and disposal. In fact, in Vietnam only industrial and medical wastes are required to be separated at source into two categories (ordinary waste and hazardous waste) that are to be collected and treated separately. For other types of wastes, there is no mandatory regulation on sorting at source. People are still mixing all their domestic solid waste into one large plastic bag waiting to be collected. And sorting waste at source is still not a habit in the country, which causes more trouble for further higher treatment technology such as composting, biogas plant, and also recycling. This creates a burden in the step of recycling as waste needs to be separated further at the treatment plants. And this results in the increase of workers needed at the plants just to sort different types of waste for later purposes, for example, composting or incinerating.

At-source household solid waste sorting has not yet become a popular practice in Vietnam, but rather has only been experimented on household garbage under some pilot projects in major cities. So far, two main 3R programs have been implemented positively in Hanoi and Ho Chi Minh City, financed by international and domestic budgets. With underdeveloped infrastructure and unsystematic management, in many cases, separated wastes have been collected and disposed together, thus reducing the effectiveness of these programs, indicating that people have not taken up the habit of separating wastes.

However, some recyclable solid waste has been sorted by households and garbage collectors to sell to recycling craft villages. Spontaneous sorting of recyclable solid waste is continuously carried out. Recycling and reuse are mainly done by the private sector (e.g., waste pickers, collectors, garbage truck helpers, scavengers, etc.), and occurs along the waste stream from the generation to the final disposal step (Figure 1). The recyclable waste fractions can be collected at source (households, building, markets, etc.), garbage storages, collection and transfer stations (meeting points), and at the dump sites. However, no official system is in place, therefore, recycling in

Figure 1 A Scrap Collector in Hanoi

Vietnam can be called "unofficial recycling." The fractions collected include cardboard, plastics, newspapers, scrap paper, glass bottles, scrap metals, etc. After collection, these materials are sent to the recycling centers.

Improving institutional effectiveness, monitoring, and enforcement

Although the country's institutions, policies, and legal systems on solid waste management have made remarkable progress, they are still insufficient, inappropriate, or overlapping. There are no consistent and comprehensive regulations for national solid waste management.

Vietnam faces institutional challenges to the effective waste management from the national to the provincial levels and the management of waste varies from one place to another. Besides, the regulation suffers from major gaps in enforcement and weakness of institutional framework, such as unclear mandates, fragmented and overlapping roles of various government agencies, and limited interagency coordination, as well as insufficient legal documentation system: overlapping, incomplete and inconsistent and examination and inspection for legal enforcement are still limited. Environmental policy enforcement is not strong enough, and ineffectiveness in environmental management tools exists.

Some policies have been issued but lack in guiding documents for implementation, which leads to ineffective execution, making them impossible to come into practice. The ineffective implementation is shown by the failure to strive for set-out environmental targets. Currently, the legal documents regulating key issues on solid waste management including human resources, organizational structures, professional qualifications, technical guidelines, etc., are inadequate, leading to difficulties in implementing the solid waste management in reality, especially the hazardous waste management.[6]

In addition, the examination and inspection for legal enforcement are still limited. The sanction provisions for environmental protection violation activities on solid waste are not strong enough for deterrence, and the weak enforcement leads to the failure in meeting the practical requirements of effective management.

Low awareness on integrated management of solid waste

There is still low awareness and sense of responsibility of leadership at different levels, as well as businesses and communities, in relation to integrated solid waste management (Figure 2). Focusing mainly on economic growth and profit making, management agencies and businesses still neglect environmental requirements in their activities including waste reduction, reuse, and recycling measures. Solid waste prevention and reduction are not yet widely practiced and promoted, especially in daily lives. Communities are still not aware of the benefits of at-source solid waste sorting and waste reduction.

Shortage of an adequate financial investment

Financial investment for waste management in Vietnam is quite low, which does not meet the demand and is not equally allocated. The main source comes from the state budget and more than 90% of it is

---

[6] N. P. Thanh and Y. Matsui, "Municipal Solid Waste Management in Vietnam: Status and the Strategic Actions," *International Journal of Environmental Research* 5 (2, 2011): 285–296.

Figure 2 Solid Waste is Dumped Directly into the River Bank Which Runs Along the Nhue River in Hanoi

allocated for waste collection and transportation while the budget for waste treatment is very low, mainly for landfilling. The solid waste management charge is quite low, about 21,000 VND ($0.9) per household per month in urban areas and 16,000 VND ($0.7) per household per month in rural areas, averaging around 0.5% of household expenses. The total collected charges can cover less than 60% of the total waste management cost and in some municipalities it covers only 20–30% of the cost.[7]

Technology transfer and information exchange

The use and transfer of environmentally sound appropriate technologies offer opportunities for more efficient waste management. There is also a need to adopt Cleaner Production technologies that could help minimize industrial waste and can have a much higher payback. The international organizations play an important role in the

[7] MONRE. *National Environment Report 2018: Solid Waste.* 2018.

identification and dissemination of those new and promising technologies in sanitation sector. The establishment of a global network among interested parties to facilitate the exchange of information about these technologies would be very helpful. Opportunities for strengthening South–South cooperation and supporting partnership in the sector between developing and developed countries should be explored.

Proposing Action for the Development of Solid Waste Management in Vietnam

Recommendations

Recent rapid urbanization, industrialization, and economic development have caused a significant increase of MSW generation in Vietnam. However, there is a lack of resources for MSW management such as finance, infrastructure, and manpower at present. The continuous increase of service demands combined with the lack of resources is putting a huge strain on the existing MSW management systems.

Currently, at the level of MSW generation and collection, there is no separation activity at source of compostable waste from the other non-biodegradable and recyclable waste. Thus, proper implementation of source separation would lead to better options and opportunities for scientific disposal of waste. It seems that waste minimization will continue to be one of the major challenges faced by Vietnam and needs to be implemented more strictly. At present, there is no limitation on the quantity of MSW that may be generated.

The convenience of waste discarding, to a certain extent, is also responsible for the increasing MSW generation. It is, therefore, important to call for discipline and good social norms, and to frequently implement the environmental protection campaigns for raising the public awareness and self-consciousness with respect to MSW management.

A majority of solid waste of urban areas is being disposed at open dumping sites and unsanitary landfills in an uncontrolled manner.

Such unscientific disposal practices have led to adverse impacts on all components of environment, community health, and social-economic development. Thus, it is necessary to upgrade the existing open dumping sites and unsanitary landfills to sanitary landfills in a phased manner. Landfills should be restricted to non-biodegradable, inert waste, and other waste that are not suitable either for recycling or for biological processing. Composting has become more popular in Vietnam. However, in order to make the application of this technology successful, a stable market for it is needed.

Proposing action

Increasing waste generation due to rising population and waste generation rate has become a challenge for Vietnam government to establish proper MSW management. Recently, MSW management in Vietnam has started paying serious attention to different levels of governments as well as the community. Weak waste management is a common growing problem faced by the developing countries. There is a need for specific action at the international level to establish, inspire, and encourage new forms of cooperation, partnership, and coordination at all levels, in order to contribute effectively to the provision and improvement of waste management services:

- Review and adjust the orientation and strategy for environmental protection to suit the actual situation from now to 2025 and after 2025.
- Promulgate appropriate mechanisms to promote technology development policies (including product production technology and waste treatment technology) in the direction of minimizing the amount of waste generation, and increasing the recycling rate and reuse for each type of specific waste, which are suitable to the conditions of Vietnam.
- Furthermore, as a matter of fact there is still the existence of many unofficial, open, and unhygienic dump sites, the government as well as local authorities need to promote the upgrading of those sites. Making those unofficial sites into sanitary and official

dump sites that operate under close administration of local authorities is another solution for illegal dumping, which impacts negatively on locals' health and their living quality.

- Reduce environmental damage. Proper practices such as leachate prevention and landfill gas collection are also needed to be applied as without these actions, the consequences have already been observed in the form of cancer around landfill sites. It is necessary for the government to create a legal framework according to which practices need to be applied in landfills in order to protect the surrounding environment and residents.
- Strengthen and diversify investment sources for waste management and treatment; maintain the sustainability of investment sources to ensure the operation and maintenance of the waste collection and treatment systems.
- Last but not least, promoting sorting at source is very important. The fact that sorting at source is not carried out at a proper rate in Vietnam increases the price of recycled products on the market as the company needs to pay more to the workers to sort the waste at the input step. Those models that have been tried in some parts of large cities need to be implemented in other parts of the country. Public campaigns to raise the awareness of recycling and also education in schools for kids are some of the methods that help to form the Vietnamese' habit of separating waste at source.

Conclusion

The strong economic growth and urbanization rates in the last decade in Vietnam have pushed the issue of solid waste management to the forefront of environmental challenges which the country must contend with if it is to continue on the path to industrialization. The amount of solid waste that the urban populations are projected to produce necessitates actions from the government in a dire way. Clearly, the current solid waste management system is unsatisfactory and needs to be addressed in an effective way.

The Government of Vietnam has made successful strides in environmental protection in recent years for the sake of sustainable development. Solid waste management should focus on selecting a suitable solid waste management model and technology (CTRSH) based on learning from other countries' experiences. Vietnam needs to assess the advantages, disadvantages, and shortcomings of the proposals, recommendations, and solutions to strengthen the management of domestic solid waste in the coming years. It is important to sort solid waste at source, reuse waste water, and develop consistent environmental policies from the beginning.

https://doi.org/10.1142/9789811225222_bmatter

Appendix I: Report on the NACT Working Group on Regional Cooperation for Sustainable Energy Development*

Background

1. NACT Vietnam and NACT China co-hosted a working group (WG) meeting on the topic of Regional Cooperation for Sustainable Energy Development on 16 April 2019 in Hanoi. The topic is highly relevant for the ASEAN and China cooperation as all parties are looking forward to energy cooperation to meet the regional and national energy demands for sustainable economic growth and development.
2. The objectives of the WG were to (i) Review the current status of respective national energy development strategy/plan as well as major opportunities and challenges to achieve the strategy; (ii) Review current cooperation mechanisms, activities in energy sector among ASEAN member states and those with China; (iii) Propose

*Co-Hosted by NACT Vietnam and NACT China Hanoi, 16 April 2019.

new directions for regional cooperation for sustainable energy development. The list of participants to this WG is given in the **Annex.**

Current Status of National Energy Plans

1. The WG underscored the importance of energy for supporting the targeted economic development. Specifically, reliable and affordable energy is fundamental to meet the need of rapid urbanization, modernization, and industrialization. These are essential to lift people out of poverty and create prosperity.
2. The WG noted that the countries share a common vision and objectives of providing sustainable energy development as mapped out in national power strategy plans. To this end, most remarkably, the countries have been focusing on ensuring secure, reliable, and sustainable power supply by diversifying power supply, improving the energy efficiency, and increasing renewable energy supply.
3. Thailand, Philippines, Vietnam, and Malaysia are adjusting their energy production structure toward higher portion of renewable energy (solar power, wind power, biomass power, and hydro power). Specifically, Thailand has developed the Power Development Plan (PDP) 2018 to replace the PDP 2015, whereby in 2037, Thailand expects to reduce the share of coal/ignite energy from 23% to 12%, and increase that of renewable energy from 15% to 20%. Recently, Vietnamese Government has adjusted the Power Plan toward higher share of renewable energy in the energy mix. The Philippines has moved to finalize by 2019 the Implementing Rules and Regulations (IRR) for its Renewable Portfolio Standards (RPS). RPS is mandated in the Philippine Renewable Energy Act of 2008. Under RPS, every distribution utility is required by law to gradually increase the percentage share of renewables in its electricity mix. The Department of Energy has proposed an additional 1% increase each year, and this number is expected to be finalized in the forthcoming IRR. To avoid sanctions, distribution utilities that are unable to meet the standard will have to buy renewable energy certificates from the other utilities who exceeded the standard. Vietnam's renewable energy

production capacity (excluding large hydro) in 2030 was planned to double from 13,700 MW in Power Plan VII (2011) to 27,420 MW in Power Plan VII adjusted (March 2016). The Plan was later updated to more than 50,000 MW registered by November 2018. Malaysia's 11th Plan focuses on encouraging sustainable energy use to support growth. It sets out five strategies including market settings, energy security and growth in oil and gas, and electricity, energy diversification, efficiency, and sustainability.

4. In China, the 19th National Congress of the Communist Party of China raised the construction of ecological civilization to a new height and regarded it as one of the goals of 2050. The realization of this goal requires strong institutional reforms including the reform of the power system, promotion of renewable energy; enhancement of energy transformation at local level and government's leadership and supervision. In the field of renewables, China focuses on developing higher efficiency, lower cost, more flexible wind energy, solar energy technology, biomass energy, geothermal energy, ocean energy utilization technology, renewable hydrogen energy production, and heating technology.
5. In Singapore, to meet the objectives of energy efficiency and reliability, the Singapore government ventured into solar and other alternative fuels. The government has implemented this objective in some of its large-scale projects. The Government invests and incurs all costs of installing solar batteries into the Housing Development Board. Since 2017, Singapore has installed solar batteries at 1,218 houses and 49 Government agencies. It is also on target to install solar power in 5,500 HDB blocks by 2020.
6. In the Energy Vision to 2030, Laos focuses on ensuring sufficient and stable supply of electricity for domestic consumption, integrating and engaging in power exchange with neighboring countries and regions, and developing the energy and mining sectors to make sure it is in parallel with the protection of green and fresh environment. Cambodian energy sector has made many positive progresses to better meet domestic demand. In 2016, the amount of imported electricity decreased, accounting for only 22% in total electricity consumption, compared to 60% in the 2009–2010

period. In 2017, 81% of villages in Cambodia could access electricity network. Myanmar is among the countries which have the lowest power consumption level (ranked 134 in 143 countries). The number of Myanmar households with access to the electricity grid accounts for only 32% of total households. Myanmar needs about $30–40 billion in the next 15–20 year period to develop its energy sector and this amount is expected to come mainly from foreign investment.

Regional Cooperation in Energy Development

1. Regional energy cooperation in ASEAN dates back to more than 20 years, starting with the harmonization of legal regulations and framework in order to establish and connect the regional transmission system. In 1997, leaders of ASEAN countries proposed the ASEAN Power Transmission Line initiative, which introduced numerous transmission lines such as those between Vietnam and Cambodia, Vietnam and Laos, Laos and Thailand. Meantime, although the initiative of building a trans-ASEAN gas pipeline has been proposed for many years, this has been implemented only at a limited level. At the regional level, ASEAN member countries have been planning to develop GMS and ASEAN power grid to enhance the energy interconnection and cooperation.
2. At a broader level, the WG noted that there have been mechanisms to strengthen cooperation in energy sector between China and ASEAN Member States, such as ASEAN+3 (China, Japan, and Korea) Minister on Energy Meeting, East Asia Summit Energy Ministers Meeting, China–ASEAN Science and Technology Partnership Program.
3. At the bilateral level, the WG noted that there have been several cooperation initiatives between China and individual ASEAN Member States. Some examples were wind power project agreement between Myanmar and the China Three Gorges Corporation in 2016, MOU for wind power cooperation between Vietnam and China. China has worked with Laos to develop the latter's national power infrastructure, with an end to connect China's

grid network with that of Vietnam, Laos, Myanmar, Thailand, and Cambodia.

Opportunities for Regional Cooperation

1. The WG noted that China and ASEAN member states have great opportunities for cooperation as both parties have shared objectives of enhancing energy efficiency and increasing the uptake of renewable energy. ASEAN has set the objectives for the Action Plan phase I (2016–2025) to increase the component of renewable energy to 23% by 2025. China has implemented the energy cooperation framework within the Belt and Road (BRI), expanding the international cooperation in conventional energy and non-conventional energy and renewable energy. China has established 56 bilateral energy cooperation mechanisms, 19 multilateral energy cooperation mechanisms, and signed more than 100 energy cooperation agreements. Since 2003, China has invested $66 billion on the Southeast Asia's energy sector, accounting for 48% of total China's investment in this region. Thus, China and ASEAN member countries have great potential to tap on energy cooperation, especially renewable energy.
2. The production cost of many renewable energy sources has declined sharply and steadily over the past few years, creating favorable conditions for the sustainable energy development for countries in the region. It is shown that in the Philippines, rooftop levelized cost of energy is cheaper than any distribution utility or electric cooperative anywhere in the country. This declining trend is expected to continue even further in the future. The Philippines reached this landmark event earlier than other countries because it had the highest electricity rates among the countries that attended the meeting. With the declining trend in solar prices expected to continue even further into the future, other countries will soon reach this landmark, too.
3. Digital technology and Internet of Things open new areas for cooperation to enable digitalization of the energy system that leads to higher energy efficiency.

Challenges

1. Besides, the WG noted three categories of common challenges in energy development and energy cooperation in the region. The first category of challenge is the fiscal and financial barriers, especially for renewable facilities. Most countries still have limited financial resources to invest in renewable energy when the initial cost of investing in this kind of energy is still high. At the regional level, countries face shortage of financial capacity as the region needs approximately $2.7 trillion for investment by 2040, in which nearly $400 billion is needed for renewable energy for the period of 2016–2030.
2. The second category of challenge is technological barriers. Infrastructure is often not available to deploy, transmit, and distribute renewable energy. In addition, countries lack innovative, sustainable energy generation technologies to increase energy efficiency.
3. The third category of challenges is the absence of institutions, policy and legal regulations to promote energy investment and trade, foster market for energy, and encourage engagement of private sector. In some countries, fossil fuel energy is still subsidized by the state. For most countries, fossil fuel energy prices do not take into account its environmental impacts. Besides, ASEAN and China have no common regulations or agreements on investment in the energy sector to protect investors while there are still numerous barriers in market access with regard to energy sector.

Recommendations

1. Due to the significance of energy for the regional development, as well as the challenges that the region is facing and potentials for cooperation between ASEAN and China, the WG noted some suggestions for further ASEAN–China energy cooperation as follows:
   (i) Facilitating renewable energy development and sharing experiences, lessons learnt, and capacity building to improve

the regional competitive advantages in order to attract investment;

(ii) Improving technology transfer to enhance efficiency in energy supply and demand, especially renewable energy technology;

(iii) Harmonizing financial and legal framework to facilitate energy trade and sustainable energy investment, improving the tariff system, and favorable market conditions for energy development;

(iv) Developing regional grid network from the current cross-border grid networks such as those between Vietnam and Cambodia, Vietnam and Laos, Laos and Thailand;

(v) Cooperating in developing and exploiting alternative options such as biomass gasification and hydrogen gas.

https://doi.org/10.1142/9789811225222_bmatter

Appendix II: Report of the NACT Working Group on Environment Protection in ASEAN and China: Challenges and Cooperation*

Background

1. The Network of ASEAN–China Think-tanks (NACT) Singapore and NACT China co-hosted a working group (WG) meeting on "Environment Protection in ASEAN and China: Challenges and Cooperation" on 17 May 2019 in Singapore. The meeting recognized that ASEAN countries and China face prevalent environmental problems in air, land, and water as they achieved impressive gains in economic development. Serious environmental degradation is a threat to people's well-being, the flora and fauna, and the sustainability of economic development.
2. The objectives of this WG are: (i) to better understand ASEAN member states' and China's environmental protection issues in terms of air, land, and water pollution; (ii) to identify ASEAN member states' and China's major environmental challenges and experiences

* Co-hosted by NACT Singapore and NACT China 17 May 2019, Friday.

in policy formulation and implementation; and (iii) to recommend various approaches to promote mutually beneficial environmental collaboration among ASEAN member states and China.

3. To achieve these objectives, this WG focuses on two main themes. First, how does each respective country in the "Ten Plus One" (10+1) framework address multiple problems of air, land, and water pollution (rivers and sea). Second, what are the prospects of cooperation within ASEAN and between ASEAN and China in resolving some of these environmental problems. Ideas on the second theme were generated and presented as recommendations in the following section.
4. Under the first theme, there are mainly three common challenges faced by the countries. First is the problem of waste management. Improper disposals and non-functioning waste management not only aggravate living conditions but they also cause other forms of pollution, such as water and air. Second, several countries raise concerns about their ineffectiveness in raising public awareness of environmental protection. Third, the lack of tools and means for implementation of environmental policies has posed an obstacle to many countries' efforts.
5. While countries like China and Vietnam are facing increasing pressures in striking a balance between economic development and environmental protection, Myanmar's main cause of environmental degradation is underdevelopment. The lack of capital and technical resources to resolve environmental problems in ASEAN's developing countries has also in turn held back economic and social developments. These common experiences shared by various countries corroborate the fact that environmental protection goes hand in hand with sustainable and holistic development of countries.

Recommendations

1. The WG reiterates the importance of environmental protection in sustainable long-term socio-economic growth and development in ASEAN and China. With this focus in mind, the WG makes the

following recommendations to further promote cooperation in environmental protection at the "10+1" level:

(a) That ASEAN and China forge a community of environmental protection and cooperation regionally and globally.
(b) ASEAN and China should regard the environmental protection issue a priority when pursuing economic development.
(c) ASEAN should also align their environmental protection goals with ASEAN's Sustainable Development Goals (SDGs) and seek synergy with China's Belt and Road Initiative (BRI).
(d) In the spirit of regional and international cooperation, and to ensure environmental sustainability, Chinese investment in ASEAN, particularly the BRI, should seek to align its strategies with ASEAN's SDGs.
(e) In recognition of development gaps between countries, the better-endowed states and societies should share their information, expertise, technology, and resources to promote regional environmental protection and cooperation.
(f) China and ASEAN should strengthen communication and cooperation on both sides among government agencies, entrepreneurs, research institutes, researchers, and associations in environmental protection industry, by organizing conferences and workshops on China–ASEAN environmental protection cooperation regularly, as well as by building a platform for sharing experiences and for promoting technology transfers among enterprises in China and ASEAN.
(g) China and ASEAN should develop a comprehensive training for "10+1" environment management personnel to enhance their capability in policy formulation and implementation of environmental protection.
(h) Both sides should cooperate to enhance public education and participation in environmental protection in ASEAN and China.
(i) It is imperative that respective ASEAN countries affected by the transboundary haze pollution problem draft a national framework or plan of action and law in accordance with the ASEAN Agreement on Transboundary Haze Pollution.

(j) Youths from ASEAN and China could be recruited for activities sponsored by the ASEAN–China Green Envoys program, in order to boost cooperation network among regional youth for greater public participation and heightened awareness.
(k) To encourage the use of biodegradable plastics as an alternative and to phase out single-use plastics.
(l) China and ASEAN could jointly present annual awards to cities, towns, and villages that are most environment-friendly. The awards are a recognition of and encouragement to local governments, enterprises and citizens for being environmental role models.
(m) To promote sustainable agriculture and plantation.
(n) To support the ASEAN Smart Cities Network (ASCN) initiative by engaging efforts with other smart/green Chinese cities.
(o) To study the sustainability and practicability of adopting a common environmental standard in the future for an ASEAN–China community of environmental protection and cooperation.

Lightning Source UK Ltd.
Milton Keynes UK
UKHW021101190121
377306UK00001B/86

9 789811 221798